A MATTER OF EQUALITY

The Life's Work of Senator Don Oliver

The Honourable Donald Oliver

NIMBUS PUBLISHING LTD.
— NIMBUS.CA —

Nimbus Publishing Limited
3660 Strawberry Hill Street, Halifax, NS, B3K 5A9
(902) 455-4286 nimbus.ca

Printed and bound in Canada
NB1593

Editor: Jon Tattrie
Editor for the press: Angela Mombourquette
Cover design: Heather Bryan
Cover photo: Tobin Grimshaw
Interior design: Jenn Embree

Except where indicated, all photos are from The Honourable Donald Oliver's personal collection.

Library and Archives Canada Cataloguing in Publication

Title: A matter of equality : the life's work of Senator Don Oliver
Names: Oliver, Donald H., 1938- author.
Identifiers: Canadiana (print) 20210248491 | Canadiana (ebook) 20210248513 | ISBN 9781774710203 (hardcover) | ISBN 9781774710210 (EPUB)
Subjects: LCSH: Oliver, Donald H., 1938- | LCSH: Legislators—Canada—Biography. | CSH: Black Canadian legislators—Biography. | LCSH: Lawyers—Nova Scotia—Biography. | CSH: Canada—Politics and government—1984-1993. | CSH: Canada—Politics and government—1993-2006. | CSH: Canada—Politics and government—2006-2015. | LCGFT: Autobiographies.
Classification: LCC FC631.O45 A3 2021 | DDC 971.064/7092—dc23

Nimbus Publishing acknowledges the financial support for its publishing activities from the Government of Canada, the Canada Council for the Arts, and from the Province of Nova Scotia. We are pleased to work in partnership with the Province of Nova Scotia to develop and promote our creative industries for the benefit of all Nova Scotians.

Praise for A Matter of Equality

This brilliantly written book chronicles Don Oliver's lifelong influences and distinguished contributions toward social justice and equality....This is a book of seasoned scholarship that is accessible, spiritually sensitive, and constructive. In presenting both his maternal and paternal family histories, it shows Don himself and his family members as nation-builders contributing to Canada's evolving democracy, and it blends their contributions to provincial, national, and international historic events with contemporary issues....

Don Oliver is a statesman of integrity and an authentic leader who is ethical and just, and this book is a reflection of his lifetime dedication and unselfish service to building a more inclusive Canadian society. – *Sharon D. Brown Ross, community social justice advocate; former senior manager, federal public service*

Don Oliver takes us on a delightful journey from his childhood as the son of a proud custodian at Acadia University to becoming the first Black man appointed to the Senate of Canada to rubbing shoulders with President Obama in the Oval Office. He has been a singular towering force in making the business case for diversity in the public and private sectors, and he's backed it up with empirical data. In my association with Don over decades, as banker to parliamentarian and as a good friend, I have experienced his determination, his intellect, his wit, and his humanity. This must-read book captures all of these attributes with grace and insight. – *Bill Downe, former president and chief executive officer, BMO Financial Group*

Suppose you want to enhance your understanding of a visionary and trailblazer who has relentlessly broken down barriers and contributed to making Canada a more equitable place. In that case, *A Matter of Equality* should be on your required reading list. Don Oliver recounts his journey through life and public service in a profoundly moving and inspiring way with clarity and purpose. It is not only the story of a remarkable person, it is also the history of Nova Scotia and Canada.
– *Denise Allyson Cole, Public Servant / Deputy Minister*

❖

I dedicate this book to those members of my family who have passed on.

My mother and father, Helena and Clifford Oliver, did not have an opportunity to attend university. If they had, they would have used their education and their innate values of kindness and tolerance to make significant contributions to making Canada a better place.

Sadly, my sister Eugenie and my brother David died much too young. Had they survived, they, too, would have used their immense intelligence, personal charm, kindness, and love to give a world in pain HOPE.

I thank them all warmly for their influence, and for inspiring me to make my life a matter of equality.

❖

CONTENTS

THE RIGHT HONOURABLE BRIAN MULRONEY

I HAVE KNOWN DONNIE OLIVER FOR ABOUT FIFTY YEARS. Following our first meeting, we soon became friends, and from Montreal I witnessed with admiration and great personal satisfaction his steady rise in Halifax's legal and business circles.

For a Black Nova Scotian in the 1950s and '60s, this was no small accomplishment. Indeed, as a student at St. FX during that period, I had already come to the view that Black Nova Scotians would rank high on a dubious list of the most discriminated-against Canadians in modern history.

This book tells the gripping story of the rise of a poor Black family in the village of Wolfville in the Annapolis Valley of Nova Scotia, where Donnie was born in 1938. His mother was a talented musician and seamstress, and his father worked as a janitor, general labourer, and farm manager at Acadia University, a Baptist school of high repute that played a key role in the ultimate success of the entire Oliver clan.

My contact with Donnie intensified as we found ourselves active in Young Progressive Conservative activities. Donnie was elected to many positions of high responsibility and was widely appreciated for his unshakable integrity and his calm demeanour that had defused many crises in the exciting wild west of YPC politics in those days.

And yet, I remember him even more during those years as a fighter for equality and fairness in Canada, with special emphasis on the sorry situation of his Black brothers and sisters in his beloved Nova Scotia.

Because of his growing reputation in this area I was especially honoured when he chose to endorse me for party leader in 1976 and 1983.

I had learned over the years that appointments by a prime minister can have a double impact—substance and symbolism—especially where minority communities are involved. When I became prime minister, I tried to utilize the practice to strong effect.

I appointed Lincoln Alexander as Ontario's first Black lieutenant-governor.

I appointed Julius Isaac as the first Black chief justice of the Federal Court of Canada.

Dr. David Chen, a leading Chinese Canadian from Vancouver, was similarly appointed as lieutenant-governor of British Columbia, as was Yvon Dumont, who became the first Métis to be elevated to the position of lieutenant-governor of Manitoba.

And so on.

In 1990, a vacancy in the Senate of Canada arose in Nova Scotia. The lobbying was intense and the names of some extremely good and prominent people were put forward.

As I scanned the list of candidates, I instinctively knew that this would not be a difficult decision. I told my staff to arrange an immediate call with Donnie Oliver. Our conversation that day is faithfully recorded in his book.

Donnie Oliver was to become the first Black man in Canadian history to be appointed to the Senate of Canada. I knew that day that Canada and the cause of equality would be the principal beneficiaries of this appointment, because Donnie Oliver would bring enlightened leadership and unrelenting commitment to this noble cause. And for the next twenty-three years that is precisely what he—the Honourable Donald Oliver, member of the Senate of Canada—did.

The last time I met with Donnie and his lovely wife, Linda, was on September 18, 2019, for the official opening of the Brian Mulroney Institute of Government at St. FX University in Antigonish, NS. His health had been failing for some time, but he was his old happy, charming self. My last glimpse of him that day was sitting in the exact replica of the prime minister's office at the Institute with a big smile on his face.

I wonder if he had noted that there are now seventy-six scholarships, bursaries, and financial awards provided annually to Black Nova Scotians at St. FX alone, a record for the province, inspired in large part by Donnie Oliver's leadership and courage over so many years.

GEORGE ELLIOTT CLARKE, 7TH PARLIAMENTARY POET LAUREATE

THE LESSON OF DON OLIVER'S SCINTILLATING LIFE IS THAT Equality is the prerequisite for the irradiating incarnation of Excellence—like the birth of a supernova amid a cluster of equally brilliant stars. The lesson is fleshed out as the grandson of once-enslaved Virginians makes his way from pastoral farm boy to cub reporter, from jazz trumpeter to Ethiopian aid worker, from Cordon Bleu–trained chef to Tory campaign guru, and from corporate lawyer to Canadian senator. In each post, he jousts with "white privilege" (the smug face of Canadian racism), always upholding the precept, "Without widespread freedom, we cannot have a just society."

Invaluably honourable also is his unwavering pride in his African–Nova Scotian identity—his Africadian heritage—with origins out of antebellum Virginia and a genealogy of accomplished family members from roots to branches, including clergy (William Andrew White and W. P. Oliver), the historian (Pearleen Oliver), the chanteuse (Portia White), and his own parents (Clifford and Helena), all their names synonymous with Black Excellence, Black Grace, and Black Gentility. Not only that, but there is power in the author's acknowledgement of the rural—of the floral and the agricultural—as being a crucial environment for moulding character. That is an increasingly rare yet historically noble aspect of African-Canadian leadership, and it is inspiring to see it registered here, opposing the stereotype that pretends that "Black" is a synonym for "urban." Oliver's story also reminds us that it is possible for Black Canadians to relish Tory "Blue" and be truly *progressive* Conservatives; that a proud Black identity can be vaunted across the political spectrum.

In this captivating, globetrotting memoir, Don Oliver (whose initials say, "DO!")—the white-collar egalitarian and pinstriped activist—chats with prime ministers (Mulroney, Chrétien, Martin, Harper), meets up with presidents (JFK, Obama), converses with world leaders (Thabo Mbeki, Deng Xiaoping), and touches down in Bermuda, Barbados, South Africa, Germany, Gabon, etc. Always he is arguing for greater Black-Indigenous-People-Of-Colour (BIPOC) representation on Bay Street and on Parliament Hill. During nearly a quarter-century as the first Black Canadian man (as he emphasizes) to be appointed to the Canadian Senate, he wages an unstinting struggle to make the federal bureaucracy mirror the diversity of the Canadian people, while also raising hundreds of thousands of dollars in corporate donations to provide scholarships for Black Canadian students.

In the Senate, "DO!" heads up or backs "business-friendly" legislation such as telecommunications "reform" but also an "anti-spam" initiative. On the social side of things, he promotes ethics in governance (a perennially difficult goal to achieve), opposes South African Apartheid, forwards an anti-stalking law, and helps to establish February as Black History Month officially. Always he is a party man, yes, a true-"Blue"; and always he is bipartisan, yes, a caring human being and a Canadian patriot. In his life and work, he unites the progressive, Prairie radical, John George Diefenbaker, the slow-talking but progressive doer Robert Lorne Stanfield, the progressive Christian radical Martin Luther King Jr., and also his other mentor (besides Stanfield), the progressive anti-racist politico Lincoln Alexander. Not a bad set of role models from any perspective.

Poignantly, now in his twilight years, the congenial champion of Equality finds tranquillity in the songs and antics of birds, the love of his wife, Linda (his companion now of some forty-one years), and their adult daughter. Back home in Nova Scotia, the man who was always DO—is now taking stock of what has been done, and the result is this candid, touching, positive, affirmative, and memorable vision of his life of thoughtful, humanitarian, and Equality-minded achievement.

INTRODUCTION

WELL, IT WAS A LONG TIME COMING.

I had been thinking about some form of biography for more than a decade but had never given serious thought to trying to write an autobiography. I did not think I could find the time to dedicate to such a large project, and I frankly questioned my own writing skills. Many friends had recommended that I look for an experienced writer who might be prepared to take on the job.

As a result, over the years, I was referred to writers—many different writers. Some were well-established, great writers. When we met, I explained that I had all kinds of documents: the more than a hundred major speeches I had given; the record in Hansard of everything I had done in the Senate for twenty-three years; lists of classmates from school and university who were quite prepared to be interviewed; all my detailed newsletters; dozens of boxes and files with newspaper clippings dating back to when I was a boy; and many boxes of files filled with personal letters and documents from people who had influenced me and whom I admired.

It would not be necessary for a good journalist to guess at what had happened in my life and what had influenced me—it was all there, ready for the nimble mind of an experienced writer to pull together into one readable piece.

Nevertheless, at times it seemed like this book might not happen. In the journey to get to where we are today, I did become engaged with a couple of writers a few years back. One wrote several thousand words, but a serious health problem suddenly put a damper on his ability to write. That was most unfortunate. We decided not to proceed further.

Now as I stand back and look at this lengthy odyssey of writing, with its wandering and twisting and turning, I can understand why it has been very difficult to get this "book job" done. I needed to do a lot more fundamental thinking about who I was and who I had become. What were some of the common themes and influences that ran throughout my life? Was I driven to help people? Did I want to follow in the footsteps of my grandparents and great-grandparents in promoting tolerance and equality in the world? Did I want to go into the business world and try to make a lot of money? How significant was it, for instance, that I was Black? How big a role did that play? Was anti-Black systemic racism a driving force in my life?

In addition to sorting through those profound issues was the fact that a lot of different disciplines showed up on my profile: trial lawyer; politician and senator; fifty-year Conservative Party backroom volunteer, activist, and worker; outspoken activist against racism and discrimination against Blacks; professor of Law; businessman and investor; human rights advocate and catalyst for change; jazz musician; farmer and Christmas tree exporter; community activist for people of African descent; lover and promoter of cultural activities, including the visual and performing arts; I was even a Cordon Bleu chef. There was also an interesting and engaging diplomatic role I played in the later half of my life.

So who was I really, and what should I stress when attempting to engage a biographer? As Alfred, Lord Tennyson said in *Ulysses*: "I am a part of all that I have met; yet all experience is an arch wherethrough gleams that untravelled world, whose margin fades, forever and forever when I move." That was probably my mindset for what was required in a manuscript.

I really wanted the book to be some type of record of what I had gone through as a Black man in a white society, so others might be able to benefit from some of the lessons I learned. I wanted to explore how I, a Black boy growing up in the 1940s, '50s, and '60s in a small white university town, and who, in those early years, had learned all about in-your-face systemic anti-Black racism, had applied the positive lessons to my experiences in later life. I still believe that I am a part of all that I have met, and, surprisingly, at the age of eighty-two, the untravelled world still gleams at me to continue.

Then a new obstacle—and a new motivation—arose: I was diagnosed by the Mayo Clinic in Rochester, Minnesota, with cardiac Amyloidosis, a rare disease with no known cure. I had been given six months to live, instructed to get my affairs in order, and advised to speak with officials in palliative care. I would go on to have some good days and some very bad days. I was living on borrowed time, so something had to be done about "this book." And yet, by what certainly has to be something just a little shy of a miracle, six years later, I'm still living.

A friend, Mayann Francis, the first Black lieutenant-governor in the province of Nova Scotia, phoned me one day and, in the course of our conversation, said there should be a book that speaks to what I've contributed to Canada. When I told her I could not find a writer and had decided to try to write some words myself (I had quite a few thousand words behind me already), she said she might know of a writer who could help me structure an autobiography. She arranged for a virtual Zoom meeting with journalist and author Jon Tattrie. We met, he gave me some solid advice, and I began to write in earnest. Over the next few months I produced the more than sixty thousand words you will find in the chapters that follow.

Fortunately for me, both Jon and Mayann knew the people at Nimbus Publishing, who I soon learned had a real interest in publishing my book. After we all spoke, Nimbus hired Jon to be the editor of the first complete manuscript. What ended up on the page is me, my thoughts, my faults, my weaknesses, my feelings, and my hopes for the world as clearly as I can write them. I've tried, to the best of my ability, to accurately recall the facts—but as we all know, memory is fallible. If any of my recollections is in error, please know that the error is not intentional.

This, for better or for worse, is my story. I hope you enjoy it.

PROLOGUE

IT WAS AN EXCITING TIME TO BE IN WASHINGTON, DC.

Fragrant June flowers were blooming throughout the US capital. The Oriental poppies, with their vibrant colours, and beautiful rich peonies, blossoming with citrusy and spicy aromas, were everywhere, and seemed calming in the 84°F heat. The renewal of the White House Rose Garden had begun that spring, and it had already become a global tourist attraction thanks to its beautiful Saucer magnolias and the stunning Tom Thumb roses making statements of joy and peace.

It was June 1962. President John F. Kennedy had met with Black civil rights leaders before Martin Luther King Jr.'s famous "I have a dream" speech, and had endorsed the March on Washington, which would take place the following year. Americans from all over the country had their eyes on King to see just how strong the national support was for his dream and his cause.

Meanwhile, Rev. Dr. James H. Robinson had caught the eye of the president after the successful 1958 launch of Robinson's dream child, Operation Crossroads Africa (OCA). Robinson was a noted inspirational speaker, clergyman, and humanitarian, and OCA was a program that enabled students to do humanitarian work in various communities in Africa in the fields of agriculture, education, and health care—and to extend a hand of friendship to Africa. President Kennedy had become very engaged in Dr. Robinson's vision and they had become good friends.

On this particular day, the White House had learned there were a group of student OCA volunteers from Canada and the US in Washington for a week of orientation sessions before departing for Africa, and the president had arranged for them to come to the South Lawn.

So there I was. A twenty-three-year-old Black law student standing with a group of other OCA volunteers at the gates of the White House, waiting to get in. We knew nothing about what was going to happen. Just being outside the gates was a moment of tremendous excitement and expectation for me.

I was secretly hoping, having come all the way from Wolfville, Nova Scotia, that I was going to see the parts of the Rose Garden that had been painstakingly designed by President Kennedy and his wife, Jackie. This could be an experience of a lifetime for a young man from the heart of the Annapolis Valley. Flowers and gardening had been a key part of my early childhood; I could not hope for more than a glimpse at one of the great gardens of the world—and maybe an opportunity to stroll around the grounds.

But I'm getting ahead of myself. More about this visit later.

Let me first remind you that my people, originally from Africa (I was en route there, and about to have a life-changing experience), had gone from slavery in the United States to a new life in Canada. My ancestors had fought for equality and justice. That fight had been the beacon that had led me through the maze of deep-seated anti-Black systemic racism I had already encountered, and would encounter throughout my life.

That fight is the story of the origins of my life's work.

It was, and has always been, a matter of equality.

Chapter One

FAMILY

I WAS BORN IN THE SMALL UNIVERSITY TOWN OF WOLFVILLE, Nova Scotia, in the heart of the beautiful Annapolis Valley, in November 1938, shortly before the start of the Second World War—a war that would cast a constant shadow over my childhood years.

The Valley was famous for its fertile lands and prosperous farms, many of which produced apples that were exported to the United Kingdom. It was home to the annual Apple Blossom Festival which, complete with parades and farm tours to see the beautiful blossoms, attracted thousands of visitors to the area each year.

Our modest family farm was located on University Avenue. Looking out the front windows of our house we could see the famous Acadia University. If you took the lengthy but meandering walk down the hill from our house, you'd soon arrive at the Minas Basin, which flowed out to the Bay of Fundy, home of the highest tides in the world.

My parents, Clifford and Helena Oliver, had five children; I was the third. Before me came two sisters, and after me another sister and a brother. My father worked as a farm manager, janitor, and general labourer at the prestigious Acadia University. His father had done the same work before him. My mother was a seamstress, a musician, and an administrative assistant; she was the executive assistant to the dean of theology at Acadia for several years.

My mother had been born in Truro, 130 kilometres away from my childhood home. She was her parents' first child; twelve more followed her into the world. When I was a child, she did not have a paid full-time job, but she worked endlessly, cooking, making all our clothing, and keeping our clothes and house clean. Even then, she found time and energy to teach music and piano lessons, and to make dresses, so we had a little more money. My mother had the credentials: she had studied piano and pipe organ at the Maritime Conservatory of Music, and was, for years, the organist and choir director at Halifax's Cornwallis Street Baptist Church. In short, my mother was the epitome of excellence in all she undertook.

She also made nearly everything we five kids wore. The girls got skirts and blouses, while the boys got shirts, vests, and pants—plus short pants for those hot Valley summers. We never left our house until she had inspected us and found us sufficiently well groomed and dressed for school or for church. She insisted we look good before entering the world beyond our farm.

My mother was busiest in May and June, as all the graduating girls in town wanted her to make a special graduation dress for them. There was always a lineup leading to 52 University Avenue for the fittings. Girls squealed with delight when they tried on the finished product. My mother never let on, but I knew she'd often been up until 2:00 A.M. to finish a dress.

She was a perfectionist. She was always looking for a way to do or to make things better. She had a vision of what each dress should be. Late one night, I sat with her in the sewing room. I was unburdening myself of some school issues while she was crafting a wedding gown for a customer. Suddenly she picked it up, clearly

From left: Eugenie, Nancy, and David, all wearing clothes handmade by their mother, Helena, who was a talented seamstress.

unhappy, and showed me how the hem was a little crooked—at least, to her finely tuned eye. My mother astonished me by completely removing the stitching and starting it all over again. She stayed up long after I'd gone to sleep, hand-sewing the dress until, by morning, it glowed with perfection.

Helena was, as you can imagine, an impeccable dresser. She often designed and sewed her own clothes for special events like family weddings. Many evenings, she'd leave our comfortable home and teach sewing and dressmaking to women from Wolfville and the surrounding area as part of an adult education class. My mother was soft-spoken and very patient, but still a perfectionist. She would spend long hours repeating the necessary steps with each student until they got it. She carried that same persistent patience to her piano lessons. And on Sunday evenings, when I was young, our entire family would gather in the living room while our mother performed on the piano my father had bought for her as a wedding present. She was brilliant. On those evenings, the piano felt like the most special object on Earth.

Music ran in the family. Portia White, the internationally famous opera star, was my mother's younger sister. My mother adored Aunt Portia and put her on a pedestal. Indeed, my oldest sister had been named Shirley Portia in her honour. As children, my mother and aunt had performed in a family quartet. My mother would laugh as she told the story. What should you call four Black singers and a Black pianist? Well, given the family name, it was the White Quartet!

She was our Aunt Portia, but to the rest of the world, she was Portia White. She performed in concert halls throughout Europe and Central and South America. She was Canada's Marian Anderson. She was the first Black Canadian woman to achieve international fame. The gift of her voice thrilled and inspired thousands and thousands of people. One of the highlights of her incredible career was her command performance before Her Royal Highness Queen Elizabeth II and Prince Philip at the Confederation Centre of the Arts in Charlottetown, Prince Edward Island, on October 6, 1964. It was an overwhelmingly powerful moment to witness.

But she packed halls in Nova Scotia first. In the small town of New Glasgow, people filled the hall to take in her astonishing repertoire, which ranged from classical to spirituals to folk. She sang in five different languages. She received many ovations and requests for encores. That evening was an incredible success.

When it was all over she went, exhausted, to the nearby Norfolk Hotel, the largest accommodation around, and was politely told they did not admit Black people into their hotel—the hotel was for white people only. They wouldn't break bread with her. It was a real slap in the face. Now, doesn't that sound like a scene out of the Deep South? Portia met that systemic anti-Black racism throughout her professional career. Fortunately, on that night, one of the ladies from the local Baptist church invited Aunt Portia to her home. They provided a bedroom where she got a good night's sleep, but no one came out to protest.

On one wonderful occasion Aunt Portia visited us in our home.

A number of people in the university town wanted to meet Portia, or at least to see her or hear her sing, so my parents invited a few guests to our home for a musical treat. They included the dean of theology and the president of Acadia University. My mother opened the evening with a short Chopin étude, then accompanied Portia on a variety of pieces from an operatic repertoire, and ended with a couple of Negro spirituals. What an incredible night—at least for the adults. We kids had been sent upstairs and warned to stay upstairs in order to make room for the guests.

Despite being banished, I peered through the bannisters and listened to this heavenly experience. There were times when Portia was singing that I thought I could feel a tremor in the house because of the incredible power of her colossal contralto voice.

Portia had made her musical debut at the age of six in her father's church choir. At seventeen she was teaching school and taking voice lessons. When she won the Helen Kennedy Silver Cup at the Nova Scotia Music Festival, the Halifax Ladies' Musical Club granted her a scholarship to the Halifax Conservatory of Music. Aunt Portia was a natural contralto, but at the age of eight she sang as a soprano in an Italian opera, *Lucia di Lammermoor*. In 1930, she took voice lessons in Halifax as a mezzo-soprano. And in 1939, while training with

Ernesto Vinci at the Halifax Conservatory of Music, she began to sing as a contralto. That contralto voice was the deep, rich, sonorous voice I heard in my home. It was really so big and so powerful.

Aunt Portia ended the little recital at our home with "Let Us Break Bread Together." The song was born among West African men and women enslaved on the plantations of South Carolina. That night, my aunt was about forty years old and near the peak of her powers. She sang,

Let us break bread together on our knees
Let us break bread together on our knees
When I fall on my knees with my eyes to the rising sun
O Lord, have mercy on me.

It was inspirational and moving. If any of the adults had turned to look up the stairs, they would have seen tears shining in my eyes. I prayed for an encore. Why should this moment ever end?

❖

My mother shared her musical talent with others in our family and there was always music in the house. Like her mother before her, she directed the choir at her local church. Her brothers and sisters—my uncles and aunts—made up most of the choir. Among me and my siblings, Eugenie played violin, Shirley, piano, while David and Nancy played guitar and many more instruments. I played the trumpet and became quite accomplished after hours and hours of lessons and practice. Shirley played a piano duet for the grade eleven graduation march when she was still in grade ten.

Our family loved books, the fine arts, and concerts. Because we were right beside the university, we had many chances to take in international performers, violinists, pianists, operas, and Shakespearean plays. My parents always encouraged us to attend these events, and we loved going to them. After all, the arts and

Young Donald Oliver was an accomplished trumpet player. Here, circa 1958, he performs as a guest entertainer at Camp Aldershot, a training facility for the Canadian Army in Kings County, Nova Scotia.

music were part of our family DNA. My mother was brilliant and could easily have been a concert pianist. Aunt Portia White was already an internationally recognized contralto. My uncle Lorne White, with Anne Murray, was a star on the long-running TV show *Singalong Jubilee*. My uncle Bill White was a composer and arranger. Indeed, all my mother's brothers and sisters were gifted musicians. We had a strong musical pedigree.

My father was equally precise and detailed in everything he did. He worked as the supervisor of the university's farm, which had cows, pigs, horses, and large gardens growing potatoes, turnips, squash, carrots, and beets; the farm had existed since early 1900s to feed the students at Acadia. He knew how to plan well in advance to ensure the university farm had proper and ample seeds for spring planting, how to prepare the soil, and how to find a market to sell the produce after the harvest. If he planted a seed, he already knew where he would sell the crop. My mother and father instilled in all their children the importance of this planning, precision, and attention to detail. We learned to put the extra effort in the first time to get things right.

My father woke early most days, eating breakfast before 6:00 A.M. and doing chores like feeding the pigs and chickens and maintaining the gardens at our home before heading to work. As the university was only a few minutes from our house, he'd come home at noon for lunch. We all came home for lunch—a huge, hot feast prepared by my mother. My father would then go back to work until late in the afternoon. He often had to work in the evening if there was a major event on in University Hall, which was the main administrative building at Acadia.

By my teenage years, I had grown extra eager to see him after work. I often waited quietly down at the administration building near the end of his day. But I wasn't just waiting to see him. Some days, when I was lucky, he would invite me to drive our car up the hill to our home—years before I had a licence. My father loved kids and was kind and gentle, and I cannot think of an occasion to drive that was withheld. When he would get home, he would rest for an hour before evening dinner, which we would always eat together as a family over lively discussions.

I got up early, too. On Saturdays, I was in charge of cleaning out the henhouse. I was responsible for bringing in the eggs each day. When necessary, I would also split the kindling and the hardwood and carry that into the house for the wood-burning stove and furnace.

A distinguished portrait of Clifford Oliver, Don's father, circa 1932.

On Saturday afternoons, I often returned to the henhouse to choose a couple of roasting hens for Sunday dinner. If you ever think your job stinks, I recommend you try submerging a dead bird into boiling water for three or four minutes. By the time the feathers

Donald Oliver as an eager and engaged young man.

come off easily, you're dealing with some of the most foul, putrid, and rank smells you can imagine. The hot water must bring out something from the oils in their feathers. Wow! I can still smell it.

Wolfville was the quintessential university town. Acadia University was the largest employer in town and many local people provided services of all types. The areas across the street and behind our property were university farm property, with orchards, pastures, hayfields, and barns with horses and cattle. There were no university buildings or homes there at that time; it was virtually all farmland. Wolfville was a playground for us, and we loved exploring the flowers and gardens, or walking on the Acadian dykes, built centuries before, where we could stand and watch the huge Bay of Fundy tides roll in and out.

In the 1930s and 1940s, students could make some extra money on the university farm by pulling weeds and later harvesting the vegetables that were grown in the fields and served in the university dining hall. But as each year passed, the university's farming operations were gradually discontinued to make way for new student residences, research and lecture halls, and new homes for professors and other staff. University Avenue finally lived up to its name when it turned its agricultural fields into the central hub of the campus.

The family home in Wolfville, built in 1921. The enclosed front porch served as Helena Oliver's sewing room and the place where she met with customers of her sewing business.

Our comfortable two-storey, three-bedroom home sat in what had become the heart of town. Our little white house seemed quite big to me as a child because we could do so many things there. We had a basement with a coal bin where we stored fuel for the furnace. There was a cold area for my mother's countless bottles of preserves, jams, and jellies; it also held large bins for winter storage of vegetables from our garden. There was also a small work area with a workbench and a few carpentry tools used for fixing things around the house.

Our space extended beyond the walls of our house to the three adjoining lots, which we used for gardening. There were, of course, barns and outbuildings for the animals. There were also a number of fruit trees around the property, including various types of apples, plums, and pears. It made for a magical childhood. My sisters and I gave each tree its own name and played with imaginary friends who seemed as real as the apples. The rough branches of one

Don's sister Nancy as a young girl.

apple tree actually grew smooth and polished after years of us sitting and sliding on them; imaginary friends would join us from time to time in our "fairy" tree.

My older sisters, Shirley and Genie, liked to tease me a lot because I was quite shy and gullible, so I certainly had to be on guard for the unexpected when playing on the slippery fairy tree. Nancy and David, my younger sister and brother, were much kinder to me and my friends—both real and imaginary.

We managed our small farm as a family. My father was well known for his own beautiful, well-kept flower gardens, which he attended to with great pride. Along with pigs and chickens, we also had a cow. My sister Shirley remembers my mother capturing the cream that rose to the top of the unpasteurized milk to make butter. She has great memories of the antique wooden press that made the pretty moulded pattern on the top.

Everyone had a job, or more accurately, several jobs. In addition to cleaning out the henhouse and collecting and carrying in the eggs, I also had to clean out the pigpens and put down fresh bedding. I had to put on my pig-pants for that smelly job. Once I stepped into the muddy pen, the pigs would run around and rub against me as though they wanted to play. I always tried to remember to give them food or swill first so they wouldn't try to knock me over. Those pigs got very pushy and unpredictable, and I always had to be sensitive to my limitations when I was around them. That was particularly true when it was time for them to become the pork and bacon for the household. It seemed that they could sense their end was near and they berated me with a high-pitched squealing noise that was so different from their normal sounds I found it unnerving.

Fortunately, I did not participate in slaughtering the pigs and was therefore able to avoid the tedious and smelly process of skinning and butchering the animals. We hired a local man, expert in smoking, to prepare the large hams and bacon for us. He would also cut and wrap the roasts, the chops, the steaks, and the short ribs. Then my father would take over. I would marvel at him as he confidently put the pork hocks—the feet—into a special brine consisting of, among other things, vinegar, salt, sugar, and secret spices, all brewed in a large crock. It was a recipe carried over from my family's slavery days, where they would be lucky to get the feet, knuckles, and head of an animal. They'd had to make the most of it and my father still loved to eat pig-foot souse.

❖

My maternal and paternal grandparents had a lot in common: both came from families enslaved on plantations in Virginia and Maryland in the United States.

William White, my mother's father, had been born free in Virginia on June 16, 1874, almost exactly nine years after the United States ended slavery. His parents had been enslaved, and they helped my grandfather make the most of his freedom. William learned to read and write at a young age and his talent and hard work caught the eye of a white Baptist missionary from Nova Scotia named Helena Blackadar. She had travelled to Washington, DC, to teach Latin and mathematics at Wayland Seminary, a "preparatory school for colored boys." My grandfather's obvious intelligence, engaging personality, and sparkling wit appealed to her and she invited him to travel to Canada to study at Acadia University.

"Would your Acadia University admit a coloured boy?" my grandfather asked her in response. She didn't know, so she wrote to the university. They responded that there were no racial barriers to his entry. In fact, Edwin Howard Borden from Truro, Nova Scotia, had in 1892 become the first person of African descent to graduate from Acadia University. He was one of the first people of African descent to graduate from any college or university in Canada and went on to earn his master of arts at Acadia in 1896.

My maternal grandfather left the United States for Nova Scotia in 1899. He earned his bachelor's degree in arts and graduated in 1903. He later earned his divinity degree and ministered as a Baptist preacher. Over his long, distinguished career, he broke down many barriers of systemic racism and showed people the power of tolerance and equality. He was the de facto leader of all people of colour in Atlantic Canada, and he prepared the way for countless people of African descent to make progress in Canada. He never forgot the missionary who had encouraged him to pursue a university degree, and named my mother, Helena, in her honour.

My grandfather was always a major role model for me. He enlisted in the military and was the only Black non-commissioned honorary captain in the British Empire during the First World War. He served in Canada, England, and France. He served as chaplain in the all-Black No. 2 Construction Battalion of the Canadian Armed Forces during the First World War. One of his contemporaries said this about him: "More than a pastor, he was the counsellor, arbitrator, and authority for the entire coloured population east of Montreal and was seen by some as the man instrumental in bringing Nova Scotia's Black population into the twentieth century."

One historian referred to my grandfather as one of the "most significant figures" in the history of Blacks in the Maritimes. He was a visionary. In the early 1930s, he pioneered a series of popular monthly radio broadcasts of his church services. He was a great preacher with a commanding voice. These services are famous for being broadcast across Canada and to the northern United States. During the Great Depression, he launched a program to raise $2,500 a year to create trade schools in Black churches.

Moses and Adeline Oliver, my paternal ancestors, were born into slavery on a tobacco plantation in Maryland. They had a son, William, who in turn had a son named William II—the grandson of Moses Oliver. As a teen, William II moved to Sackville, NS, a suburb in the city of Halifax, to work on the farm of a distinguished botanist and chemist, Dr. George Lawson, who was further renowned for his expertise in livestock. William thrived in that job, earning a decent wage as a farm worker alongside the university professor, learning about the most recent experiments in agricultural sciences. This internship lasted eleven years. He then moved to Wolfville and worked at the Acadia Seminary for four and a half years, when he was promoted to superintendent of buildings and grounds. It was the innate Oliver desire for more education, and the patience to learn, that inspired this Black man to succeed in a time of horrendous anti-Black systemic racism.

William got a job working as a janitor at Acadia University's main administration building. He earned the trust and love of the university's president, faculty, and students alike. In January 1922, he became ill with pneumonia. The University Bulletin took note of his condition and remarked that countless students had sent "expressions of solitude from many quarters." When he died, he was buried in our family plot at Willowbank Cemetery in Wolfville.

William had a son, Clifford, in 1884. Clifford was, of course, my father. He, too, was drawn to Acadia University, but never had the opportunity to earn a degree. His mother and father struggled to raise their fifteen children, and in grade nine my father had to leave school to start working in order to assist his parents. Clifford was a short, stocky man of about five-foot-five. Thanks to farm jobs like hoeing, he was very strong, with back and arm muscles that looked like they belonged to Charles Atlas.

Clifford followed his father's footsteps and began his working career on the university farm, where he learned the skills of the trade working side by side with his father. He then rose to be the superintendent of husbandry, overseeing the campus grounds and farms. For seventeen years he drove the truck each day, doing a variety of jobs like collecting garbage from each of the many university buildings and taking it to the university dump, which was on University Avenue. He also took parcels to and from the train station and moved furniture and equipment around campus as needed. Acadia trusted him to do whatever the job required.

When William had retired, my father had taken over his work as custodian of the administration building and University Hall. It was a huge job and when I was a young child I often wondered if it was even possible to get everything done that needed to be done in that four-storey building. I would often help my father by sweeping and mopping the large entrance hallways, collecting all the garbage and papers from each of the offices and classrooms, and helping him clean out and wash down all the bathrooms. After a concert or other performance, I would go through the auditorium to help him collect left-behind programs, tissues, and other trash. We often worked until 10:00 P.M.

I also have a clear recollection of the dozens and dozens of times I had to spread green Dustbane cleaner over some of the more difficult and dirty floors because it helped to disinfect and degrease some surfaces. It would trap particles of dust before they could be scuffed or blown away. We would then sweep it all up and discard it in waste containers. The smell of the chemicals in the Dustbane can bring back memories for me even today. That's certainly where I learned that there is really no such thing as a nine-to-five workday, even for a janitor, and that in order to get ahead you had to

Acadia University's Class of 1951 voted unanimously to make Clifford Oliver an honorary life member of their class. On graduation day, he proudly donned a cap and gown and graduated with his classmates.

be prepared to put in the long hours. That lesson stayed with me my entire life.

The graduates of 1951 voted unanimously to make my father an honorary life member of their class. It must have felt a bit like an honorary degree, and on graduation day he donned a cap and gown and graduated with his classmates. It was a marvellous occasion.

He received a special citation celebrating his fifty-seven-year career at the university. "This popular gentleman was born at Scots Corner near Wolfville," it read. "As a boy (he) helped his father, who was janitor of the old University Hall for forty years, tend the many furnaces, for then each classroom had its individual stove." His classmates and university peers documented his career, starting as foreman of the farm and grounds, then as a truck driver, and lastly as a janitor keeping the campus clean and safe. "Whether in class routine or in extra-curricular activities, Mr. Oliver is always willing to lend a helping hand in any way," the citation said.

He retired in 1956. The university administration and office staff held a reception for him and presented him with a lovely gift. It was a wonderful day for my father, with everyone bubbling over with warmth and affection for him. President Emeritus Dr. Watson Kirkconnell read his original poem describing my father's long and faithful service to the university. The first letters of each line of the fourteen-line sonnet spell out "Clifford Oliver."

Sonnet for a Good and Faithful Servant

Can any match his term for length of years,
Living and working on Acadia's hill?
In eighteen-ninety-nine he learned to till
For her the farmstead, with its corn's fat ears
Feeding her students; then he shifted gears
Over to driving trucks for good or ill;
Rising at last his father's shoes to fill,
Due care he gave to U. Hall, it appears.

On fifty-seven years of earnest toil
Look back today and estimate the force
In zeal expended as the years uncoil
Voluminous and vast along their course!
Even the best of men Old Time must foil.
Receive, we pray, oats for the faithful horse!

My father always told us how important it was to stay in school and get as much education as we could. We listened. When Clifford died in 1966, our family collectively held seventeen university degrees in dietetics, medicine, law, and education. Many generations of my family believed strongly in learning, apprenticeship, and education as the way forward. We were reminded of Plato's allegory of the cave and saw education as the illumination that would lead us away from mere shadows of the suppression of slavery to the light of freedom.

Chapter Two

THE WAR YEARS

THE SECOND WORLD WAR BROKE OUT BEFORE I REACHED MY first birthday. Right outside our home in Wolfville, the once-quiet night air would squeal with air-raid sirens screaming to remind us the "nighttime blackouts" were on, and we must sit quietly in our homes with all the lights out.

As a shy young child, I was scared. These were trying moments. The sirens were really loud and seemed to go on forever. When I was old enough to wonder, I questioned: what was the approaching danger? How could I be certain the evil was not lurking just outside our house and that was why we had to turn out the lights? Should we be doing other things to protect ourselves? My parents took these exercises very seriously and so did we. Everyone had to do it. These were the routine air-raid practices for the entire province. Not one light was permitted to be on anywhere in the entire town. The curfew was real. There could not even be outdoor lighting for Christmas.

Turning three and four, I was unnerved by the radio news reports. I knew the air-raid siren was usually followed by bombs careening out of the sky, and didn't understand that we were actually very far from the front lines. It was a time of a lot of mixed, troubling feelings, some of which were hard to reconcile.

Our entire family quietly and intently sat around the radio, listening to the challenging but comforting words of Winston Churchill spelling out the Western Allies' movements against the Germans, and giving us hope. We never missed those speeches. To give us encouragement, Churchill would often repeat that they would never give up, never surrender. I sat on the floor in front of the radio and I looked up at my parents after the broadcast finished and I could see a sign of relief in their eyes. As a young child whose instincts and reactions were often modelled on his parents', I, too, felt reassured and the same sort of relief that things at least did not seem to be getting worse.

Even though we were a virtually self-sufficient family, we were still caught by the need to ration certain food supplies during, and even immediately after, the war. That included essentials like sugar, butter, cooking oils, coffee, and tea. With our gardens, animals, and orchards, and our knowledge of pickling and preserving, we had an abundance of meats, vegetables, pickles, and jams to see us through the winters, but three years into the war, when more and more essential supplies were required overseas to support our troops, rations were even put on items like clothing, alcohol, and even maple syrup.

In my mind's eye, I can still see the little yellow ration booklets issued by the Dominion of Canada that contained coloured stamps and coupons with numbers on them. My sisters and I would walk to our local grocery store—the Porter store on Main Street—when we needed sugar or tea, for instance, and we would have to pull out the yellow ration book and take an appropriate number of coupons or stamps out before we were entitled to purchase the items. In January 1942, the sugar ration dropped to only twelve ounces per person per week. But with five kids and two adults, we could manage on our sugar ration. Each person was also only allowed one quarter-pound of butter a week. That's not very much, but fortunately we had our own cow, and my mother made the butter we needed at home. We did not use every stamp and every coupon in the ration booklets, so when the war was over and the books were no longer required, we used them for playing games, for drawing, and for art projects. You had to learn to live with what you had, and if you were smart, you would be saving every possible thing you could for a rainy day. That's what my mother and father instilled in me.

Despite the war, we still had childhood fun. In late summer, we were all given a pot after dinner and told to head off to the blueberry fields to pick until our pots were full. I always tried to get one of the smaller ones. My sisters were fast pickers. They were clean pickers too. There were not a lot of green berry leaves, twigs, and weeds in their pots. Wild blueberries are much smaller, sweeter, and tastier than the ones you get in a store. Even though I was often nearly eaten alive by the mosquitoes and blackflies, I persevered because I knew that in the end there would be something tasty, succulent, and really enjoyable: my mother's homemade blueberry pie with vanilla or chocolate ice cream.

If there was any left, the next day I would have the blueberry pie with lots of whipped cream. The kitchen would be filled with the delightful aroma of blueberry muffins fresh out of the oven. The next morning, sumptuous blueberry pancakes with heated maple syrup were served. The treats also included blueberry jam, which I loved on my morning toast, a light and delicious blueberry cake, scones, plus a real Nova Scotia delight: blueberry grunt. They were all pure delights. I forgot about the bug bites I'd acquired in the blueberry field. After school, I'd splurge on my mother's homemade blueberry jam, spread on her freshly baked bread, and a glass of cold milk.

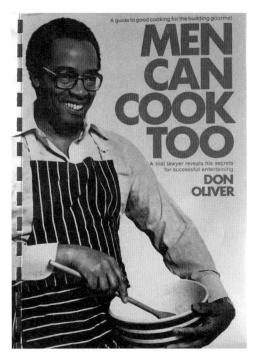

Donald Oliver always loved cooking, and in 1996 he wrote a cookbook called Men Can Cook Too. *Oliver had grown up in a household with three sisters and the title was a lighthearted nod to them.*

From boyhood, cooking was something I adored. My two older sisters studied dietetics, each with an eye to earning a BSc in home economics, and they often fell into conversation with my mother about the chemistry of cooking. One day they were talking about fatty acids and amino acids. "This is girls' talk, Donnie, it's not for you," one sister said.

I was never one to be told what wasn't for me, so I began reading everything I could about food and cooking. It sparked a lifelong passion that long outlasted a desire to one-up my older sisters. Later on, as a young man, I spent my free time buying and studying dozens of cookbooks. I even went so far as to retain a tutor for private cooking lessons in the person of Philippa Monsarrat, wife of the novelist Nicholas Monsarrat. She held cooking classes for groups that I attended in the evening. She was a magnificent cook and had a magical touch. In fact, what she taught me was "touch cooking."

A short time after taking lessons from Philippa I wanted to get even better, so I took the most advanced intensive course at Le Cordon Bleu Culinary School in London, England. I wanted to learn as much as I could about modern techniques in international cuisine from a French base, and that was certainly the school for that. I had an excellent teacher and learned a lot. We had lectures and cooking demonstrations on Cordon Bleu techniques, and we cooked something different each day. It was intensive but I found it most enjoyable because the class was small. There were twelve of us, eleven of whom were there to learn. The outlier was a young lady—a real Lady with a peerage—who arrived by way of a personal chauffeur. She had all the advantages, but lacked one—she didn't care about cooking.

A good hobby can strengthen you as a person and give you objectivity in your professional work. Cooking always made me happy. I eventually wrote my own cookbook, which went through three editions. In a lighthearted dig at my sisters, I called it *Men Can Cook Too*. It may seem a strange pairing: fighting anti-Black racism by day, making jam by night. But I found a way to combine my two passions by hosting dinners to raise money for important causes. We often raised several thousands of dollars from a single dinner to support my community, particularly the youth, as well as for other charitable causes.

❖

But perhaps I've wandered too far from my boyhood farm in Wolfville.

In 1945 the war ended. I was seven, very shy and impressionable. Students had returned to Acadia University in the fall to begin a new school year. All the usual September spectacles soon got underway, like the freshman initiation week, with all its bizarre pranks and antics. The cheerleaders were practising their routines so they could cheer on their fellow students for football games. The college band was rehearsing for the pre-game pep rallies. The entire campus was a beehive of activities.

That year, the students decided to make the semester a time of jubilation and celebration for our democracy and to show the dignity and worth of all citizens irrespective of their religious faith. Six million Jews murdered was a number too large for any of us to understand. Yet the students knew they had to acknowledge this horror.

A few hundred yards down the hill from our house, the students traditionally held their pre-game pep rallies and bonfires in front of University Hall. The cheers, speeches, and chants on this particular Friday night were designed to fire up the students for the big Saturday afternoon football game. The college band played a jazzy version of the university song "Stand Up and Cheer," and the cheerleaders, dressed alike in their college sweaters and sporting matching pompoms, encouraged everyone to sing, dance, swing, shout out, and cheer for the Acadia team.

But there had been whispers around campus that things were going to be different at this post-war pep rally. When the rally was due to start, I slipped out of the house and made my way down the hill to watch and listen. I was smaller than everyone else and alone. I made myself inconspicuous. No one seemed to wonder what a seven-year-old boy was doing out alone at a university rally.

A large bonfire had been laid and some students had built an effigy—a straw man with arms and legs. He had been placed firmly in the centre of the bonfire. Hundreds of students gathered. There were a couple of short speeches about the end of the war: freedom was preserved. The band started to play. Cheerleaders did their routines and encouraged students to chant, sing, and cheer. The music and activities got louder and louder.

The bonfire was lit. The effigy began to burn. Students yelled and cheered. The band was playing louder. Students screamed, "Down with Hitler!" as the effigy smoked and sizzled in the flames. I began to have what felt like a supernatural experience. The popping and banging of the dry wood exploding into an inferno, the roaring blaze eating oxygen, the flames leaping to the sky—it all shook my soul. It was loud and I struggled to hear everything being said.

How was this all going to end? Was this going to be like one of the miraculous stories from Sunday school? Was something totally unexpected going to happen? The band was playing, students were singing. It was getting louder and louder. There was so much going on. I was happy and sad at the same time. I was happy to be there witnessing this spectacle, but sad that the burning effigy with the straw arms and legs resembled a real person.

I didn't then know about the history of lynching and burning of Black people by the Ku Klux Klan and other white supremacists that my ancestors had feared during the height of slavery in the US and even long after freedom. But I learned something of it as those students stood arm in arm, shouting chants against Hitler over the blaring sounds of the trumpets and trombones in the band and the musical voices of the cheerleaders. This student protest had become like a nightmare to me, but I still did not want to go home. I wanted to stay to the end.

Finally the band stopped playing. The cheerleaders left for their residences. Most of the assembled students were gone. It was still and quiet. The straw man had burned bit by bit until the fire went out. Firewood to ashes. The end was nothingness. For the students, it symbolized the end of a terrifying regime and the re-emergence of Western democracy. It meant something different to me, though as a child I could not understand it. I felt sad and jubilant at the same moment. The human effigy burning amid cheering and jeering crowds troubled me, but I rationalized that if it symbolically represented something evil that had been put away so that our democracy and freedom could be preserved, then it was truly a time for jubilation. The students' strong act of protest was like a burning and cleansing of all the hatred and evil that had beset the world since 1939, about which Churchill had so often spoken.

The bonfire event opened my eyes and made a lasting impression on me. I felt the chilling knowledge of the real fragility and preciousness of our freedom. As it had been for the Jews under Hitler, so it was for Blacks living in a society of widespread, ubiquitous white privilege.

❖

We were the only Black family in that university town of nearly two thousand people. Our fundamental family creed was, "Work hard, be humble, love the Lord, and do all you can to help other people." Getting a good education for all Black people was, in addition, an essential ingredient of the Oliver DNA.

We seemed to live in harmony with the rest of society on our self-contained farm, but it was not always all sweetness and light. My father was born in, grew up in, and lived his life in an all-white environment. He always dreamed of owning his own house to raise his family. He had purchased his first piece of land in the early 1900s, in a prime area of Highland Avenue in the heart of town. But soon, whispered rumours circulated: people were threatening to burn down any house he should build there.

He did not build there and he sold that lot. He came up with a new plan to buy land at 52 University Avenue, which was then on the outskirts of town and almost totally undeveloped. For many months, he saved money until he had enough cash to buy four adjoining lots and start building a home. He spoke to one of the pillars of Wolfville whom he trusted; a white contractor named Charles Wright. He got Cecil to buy everything—in my father's name—and this time he got the property without anyone threatening to burn it down.

Cecil built the house in 1911. Cecil Wright's daughter, Rhoda, would later marry Alex Colville, a Wolfville resident who became one of Canada's most celebrated artists. Rhoda and Alex became close friends with my mother. Alex quickly recognized my mother's artistic talent, and many years later he gave a profound, moving eulogy at her funeral. "Her gifts were numerous," he said on that occasion. "She was an accomplished musician whose modesty perhaps held her back from her potential as a performer, but the same modesty made her a most effective teacher." He continued, "Helena possessed what I can only call 'grace.' As a Black woman, and living in the era to which fate consigned her, she must have been subject to intermittent, perhaps almost continuous, stress. Thinking of her, I think of Ernest Hemingway's phrase, 'grace under pressure.'"

My father had a son, my half-brother William Pearly Oliver, from an earlier marriage that had ended in divorce. William was twenty-six years older than me. He would go on to become the Reverend Dr. W. P. Oliver. In the 1940s, William's wife, Pearleen, devoted countless hours to working with government and health authorities to win the right for young Black women to be admitted to the provincial hospitals' training programs so they could earn their registered nurse (RN) designation.

Finally, the board of the children's hospital called her and asked her to select two Black women to enter the program. She gave two names, Gwennyth Barton and Ruth Bailey, and they soon started their training. This was a first in Canada. Even as they studied, the hospital chair told Pearleen there was "still no guarantee they could be admitted to intern at any of Halifax's three big hospitals" because of the racial barriers that existed there.

Both women endured two hard years of internship. Some sick patients refused their help solely because of the colour of their skin. They were sick people, indeed. But Barton and Bailey succeeded and graduated, breaking down another racist barrier and making history. More Black registered nurses followed their path. As a young man, I watched my family's work in awe and began to see the foundation for my own life's work.

My parents kept lots of books in the house and encouraged us to visit Wolfville's library. In my teenage years, I devoured books and periodicals on the National Urban League, a New York–based civil rights and urban advocacy organization, and the National Association for the Advancement of Colored People (NAACP). I wrote letters to both organizations. They wrote back and we started a lively correspondence about racism, intolerance, and discrimination against Blacks.

Racism was always somehow a little different in Canada than in the United States. While Rosa Parks would start the Montgomery bus boycott by refusing to give up her seat in 1955, Nova Scotia's Viola Desmond had already done something similar here in 1946. Desmond, a Black businessperson, challenged racism in a New Glasgow theatre by refusing to leave a "whites only" area of the Roseland Theatre. Even though she had offered to pay the difference of one cent between the cost of the upstairs and downstairs tickets, the theatre called the police and she was literally dragged out of the theatre; she received injuries to her hip and knee in the process from which she never recovered.

She was put in a jail cell overnight. The next morning, she was taken to court and charged with attempting to defraud the provincial government because of her alleged refusal to pay the one-cent tax. As a Black businesswoman from Halifax, she had wanted to protest segregated seating in New Glasgow, and officialdom there had responded with armed police and a criminal prosecution over one cent! It was a violent happening with an innocent Black woman, but it did not raise even fundamental human decency concerns with the people of New Glasgow. They were in support of the unusually violent conduct of the police and the unusual decision of the judge.

Even after the Second World War, Nova Scotia had no human rights act and there were no legal precedents against racial discrimination in hotels, theatres, or restaurants. It was just tolerated in

Canadian society. But Desmond ultimately made Canadian history by successfully challenging this gross injustice. Segregation was legally ended in Nova Scotia in 1954.

Viola and her husband, Jack, were members of the Cornwallis Street Baptist Church at the time of the incident in New Glasgow and they were ministered to by my half-brother, William, and his able wife, Pearleen. Reverend Oliver and Pearleen were astounded and deeply offended by what had happened to Viola and both became actively involved in supporting her. Pearleen counselled her and found a Black doctor to treat her injuries. The doctor immediately recommended she see a trial lawyer about the injuries to her knee and hip.

Reverend Oliver and Pearleen had founded the Nova Scotia Association for the Advancement of Coloured People (NSAACP) in Nova Scotia, and the founding directors were the deacons of their church. They used the NSAACP as the vehicle to communicate and spread the word of this injustice throughout the province, and began a fundraising campaign to raise money for a lawyer and the necessary legal proceedings. Money came in from all over the province—even more from whites than from Blacks. Reverend Oliver and Pearleen worked closely with Viola, providing support, money, counselling, and advice for more than two years. Many years later, long after her death, Desmond received a free pardon and a public apology from the premier of the province. An academic chair in social justice was established in her name at the University of Cape Breton. The government of Canada even put her image on a stamp and on the ten-dollar bill. She was the first Black person to appear on our Canadian currency.

I was acutely aware of the decisions she must have made within herself. Viola Desmond had asked herself the tough question that goes to the heart of anti-Black systemic racism: why do I have to prove that I am worthy to participate in and enjoy all the fruits that have been bestowed on the white majority by virtue of white privilege?

She did what she had to do to show she was worthy of and equal to the privilege white Nova Scotians enjoyed, and in the end, society saw where they had erred and showered her with honours for her bravery and courage.

Now that was a real Black victory. My grandfather, Rev. Dr. William White of the Cornwallis Street Baptist Church in Halifax, had himself personally helped to break down racist seating practices in Halifax theatres. It helped that he stood five feet, eleven inches tall, spoke in a strong voice, and held a commanding presence.

◆

There was nothing in our schoolbooks about the contribution Black people had made culturally, socially, and economically to Canada. But our parents taught us about how Black people, including members of our own family, had achieved great things in Canada. We grew up well aware we had relatives who were famous, distinguished Canadians who had performed in opera halls around the world and had been awarded the Order of Canada. But we also knew how hard life was for them. We knew about the times doors were slammed in their faces because they were Black. We heard stories of how they fought for tolerance and equality. We also knew about slavery and systemic racism. As a family, we were a team, and if we didn't know it at the time, we loved one another, would always support one another, and we enjoyed being together.

I was fully aware—and it was obvious for the world to see—that I was a Black boy. How, I wondered, could skin colour or pigmentation be such a sensitive and important thing in the scheme of things? Would I have to live all my life with a constant reminder that I was different from most Canadians and could not, therefore, just accept and enjoy the fruits that had been bestowed on my white friends, unless I could first prove that I was worthy?

Because the Olivers were the only Black family in Wolfville, Donald was the sole Black student in Miss Nichols's grade four class.

At times it seemed so easy. When I was engaged in stimulating discussions or playing sports and games with my classmates, I would frankly forget about the colour of my skin. I felt no different than the red-headed guy in our group, and he was accepted as just one of us. At Sunday school and Bible study at the Baptist church, I learned that God created us all equal. But it didn't take long for all of that sweet, naive thinking about equality to come tumbling down.

All five of us little Black Oliver kids encountered in-your-face racism. When we started school, every other classmate in all our grades was white, and at first some of them did not seem to know what to make of us, or even what to call us. We did have a different-coloured skin. I had curly hair. They had obviously been taught by their parents to refrain from using the N-word to us, so instead, they called us the more polite "pickaninnies." We five Oliver pickaninnies went about our business as usual and really just wanted to get a good education and get prepared for the rest of life. We could not be sidetracked by nicknames. The fact that we were constantly reminded that we were different from most Canadians could not

Eugenie (Genie) Oliver as a young woman.

Shirley Oliver's graduation photo from Acadia University, 1956.

deter us from our mission to succeed.

My sister Eugenie (Genie) was an excellent student who was at the top of all her classes in academic excellence. Learning just came naturally to her. Shirley took piano and loved working in art. (I have some of her paintings in my house today.) Nancy became a teacher and writer who had wanderlust; she lived and worked in Montreal before travelling to northern Quebec to teach in an Inuit community of nine hundred people. Later, she taught English in villages of a few hundred people in both Botswana and Swaziland in southern Africa. She also spent time in South Africa.

Genie excelled in sports and music, was a magnificent cook, and earned straight As from grade one to grade ten. But something mysterious and very odd happened in grade eleven when it came time to graduate. The grade eleven class had written all their exams. Who made the highest marks in the class? Who would get the gold medal? Genie got the marks, but not the medal. Certain leaders at the school had decided, privately, that a well-bred white boy teeming with white privilege would likely do better in society than a Black girl with no such breeding. With "gold medal winner" attached to his resume, he would smoothly progress through the corporate world. What, they must have wondered, would my sister have done with it? Could losing out on the medal even really hurt a Black girl? And so at graduation, he was called forward and given the gold medal as the audience applauded. And it did look good on his resume. My sister received the silver medal for second place.

But hold on. This story is not over. That year, Nova Scotian students took a second, higher set of exams at the grade eleven level. The mandatory provincial exams recorded not names, but numbers. The graders could not know the skin colour of the students, only their answers. Freed from racist restraints, Genie scored the highest marks in the entire province. She was the best student that year, no matter who was given the gold prize.

My brother David and I shared a bedroom. He was a wonderful guy. He excelled at sports and was always in demand for hockey. He played piano and guitar and trumpet. While I was shy and withdrawn, he had a natural warmth and charisma. If there was mischief to be made, he was often in the middle of it. He was fun to be with and became a popular kid. He also had a very sensitive side and wrote poetry. Racism hurt him and it took a heavy toll on his life. He simply wanted to go about his business in a dignified way, but a bigoted white society often wouldn't let him, and that caused him constant stress.

He persevered, married, and he and Maureen had three children. David loved being a father and enjoyed family life. Tragically, while working on his farm in Quebec, he had a bad farm accident, which compounded his long-standing asthma condition. During an asthmatic crisis, he was operated on at the Royal Victoria

David Oliver worked in the student services department at Dawson College and developed services for Black students and students from developing countries.

Hospital in Montreal; he died shortly afterward. He was just thirty-six. But his legacy was recognized. He had worked in the student services department at Dawson College and had developed services for Black students and students from developing countries. The college honoured him in several ways, including by establishing an award called the David Oliver Award, given by the Association of Dawson Professionals. Years later I met Stuart McLean, the humourist and monologist who became famous in Canada as the host of CBC Radio's *Vinyl Café*. He told me with warmth and affection that my brother David had been a very good friend of his. It was a wonderfully comforting moment for me to hear Stuart talk about David in that way.

Chapter Three

EDUCATION

THERE WAS NO OTHER OPTION. ALL MY LIFE I HAD LOOKED AT IT. My grandfather and my father, and later my mother, spent their working days there. Two of my sisters were studying in its halls, and it was clear that I would too. My next big step would be the five-minute march from my front door to the front door of Acadia University.

I had never thought of doing anything else. Going to Acadia after high school was something our family had been doing for decades. I'd had a summer job working for a construction company, and that had solidified my resolve to go to university and do something meaningful with my life.

Digging ditches was definitely not for me, but I had crystal clarity now: no more of that sort of work for me. I wanted to work with people in the community. I wanted to find the areas where my own people were hurting and to see what I could do to help. I figured an education could give me the tools to build change. I enjoyed books and reading. I enjoyed learning new things. I wanted to be able to use my education to find a cause in life where I could derive personal satisfaction from work, and at the same time give back and help others.

I had graduated from high school in 1956, but before entering Acadia, I was thrilled to be hired for the summer as a news reporter. I got a position in the big city of Halifax as a cub reporter for the *Chronicle Herald*, the largest newspaper in the province. I covered crime, fires, sports events, and slum housing, writing hard news stories and features for context. I hefted around a big camera and took photos to go with my stories. News writing is unique and didn't come naturally to me. It would often take me a few paragraphs to get to the heart of the story, only to open the newspaper the next morning and find the frantic editors had chopped the last three-quarters of my story to make it fit. I learned to get the thrust of my story in the first few paragraphs, above the cutting line. After covering a fire, I clanged out the following on my Smith Corona typewriter:

Firefighters are still on site and police are still investigating a suspicious three-alarm fire that started around midnight in Smiths Merchandise Store with no reports of injuries but with rumours of a possible robbery motive.

The newsroom was filled with old Smith Corona typewriters. I had one at home, so I already knew how to type. It was so exciting to hear the click and clatter of all the typewriters as reporters sprinted to meet deadlines. I'd peek around the room, almost laughing inside as I enjoyed the charming symphony of breaking news. The air was filled with smoke—it seemed every journalist smoked—and desks were stained with coffee and covered with half-drunk mugs. The mugs were squeezed in next to mountains of newspaper clippings, yesterday's half-read paper, and piles of folded notebooks.

I mentally compared it to the other summer job I'd had working for a construction company. My job for a couple of weeks had been pushing ready-mix cement in a wheelbarrow over to footings for a new large building. I'd dump it then return for another load, and then another—the same thing, over and over and over, day after day. It was monotonous. It was certainly strengthening my arm, shoulder, and back muscles, but after two weeks, all the footings were poured and I was assigned to another job. But I'd already decided there would be no more of this kind of work for me. I wanted to be able to work with people, to work in the community, to ferret out the areas where people were hurting, and to see what I could do to help. At the construction job, the only person being advanced was me—when I got my weekly pay cheque. No one else was in the formula. Fortunately, I had other options.

While physically easier than my manual labour job, I soon found out that journalism was mentally exhausting—for editors, for reporters, for everyone. Every day brought the pressure to fill tomorrow's newspaper, to check all your facts, and to make sure the news items didn't clash with the editorial or the financial pages. Photo editors would fill the newspaper with dramatic images, always trying to hook the public and sell papers, but to also accurately depict the stories inside. I'd finish my copy and hand it in. At first, I expected some hand-holding by a patient, wise editor who wanted to help me improve my story. But it's a big, bustling business, and no one had time for that. We had to get that newspaper on the street early the next morning. It seemed as if they printed more or less whatever I handed in.

I made some good friends in the newsroom and in other divisions of the paper. It was really educational and instructive for me to hear stories told by other reporters over a couple of beers about their lives and world experiences, which were usually so

In 1956, during the summer after he graduated from high school, Donald Oliver took a job as a cub reporter for the Halifax Chronicle Herald. *He is shown here interviewing Vice-President Thomas McDormand of Acadia University.*

vastly different from my own. I was pretty sure I was the only one who'd spent his childhood hoeing in the gardens with the black-flies, cleaning out the pigs and chickens, and carrying the eggs inside each morning.

Talking with those colleagues was where I got my first real eye-opening glimpse into how the media can play into partisan politics. A newspaper can influence the thinking of the general public on a particular public policy topic. I was a political neophyte, so I was taken aback by how close some editors were either to the premier of the province, or to a former premier, or to the most important cabinet ministers. Most journalists keep their politics to themselves, but some of the editors really wore it on their sleeves. I got a glimpse, as well, into the mysterious world of lobbying inside City Hall.

I also heard some chilling stories about policing and overt racism in Black communities during that summer of 1956. Racism was rampant in the city. There were barber shops where you could not get a haircut, restaurants that would not serve you, landlords in housing who would not rent an apartment to you, segregated schools for Blacks and whites, and even segregated cemeteries. And that was just the beginning. Blacks were excluded from jury duty, certain skating rinks, parks, and athletic clubs. Some hospitals refused to work with Black physicians. We were a province of segregation, race hatred, discrimination, and systemic anti-Black racism, all in one. But few journalists were reporting on the shocking, chilling stories of systemic racism throughout all our institutions, both public and private. There were a few pioneering Black journalists, but mostly it was white journalists who provided the news on the discrimination faced by people living in Africville, the Prestons, and in downtown Halifax.

Pretty much everyone I worked with at the *Herald* was white. My world at work and play was white. That fact did not shock me. I had, after all, come from Wolfville, where we were the only Black family in town. In our secure little university town, all the teachers, preachers, police officers, senior bureaucrats, and politicians were white. Our classmates and playmates were all white. My family and I were the only Black people. That meant, growing up, we never saw Black youth being bullied, abused, and jailed. We read about segregated schools and churches, but did not experience them. We read about our Black peers in Nova Scotia getting a bad education compared to white kids, but we didn't experience it.

We did not see the Black communities throughout the province that had half-built, shoddy housing with little winter insulation. We didn't see the poverty caused by banks and lending institutions refusing to loan money to Black families. We did not see or feel the horrid anti-Black racism in housing, employment, and education from our comfortable home in white Wolfville. We did not see Black families stuck in poverty without enough food to eat. We also didn't see any Black principals, or professors, and certainly no Black deans or presidents of universities or corporations. We did not see Black-run businesses. In Wolfville, the only Black faces we saw were our own.

So when I moved to the big city in 1956 and heard those chilling stories from my fellow reporters in a casual setting over a beer, it hurt me. I was deeply saddened and I wanted to cry from the pain. These were huge problems. I felt helpless. I realized how sheltered we'd been from the reality of many Black people in Nova Scotia. We also had so many inspiring people in our family who had fought to end racism, so I knew what to do: I would dedicate my energy toward trying to end anti-Black systemic racism in Halifax.

It did not take long for me to personally feel the sting of blatant, in-your-face racism, and I knew at that point I had to do something about it for sure. It would be years before a generation of bright Black writers and journalists started telling the true stories of racism in Nova Scotia. That would help awaken the soul and conscience of Nova Scotians, but in 1956, Nova Scotia slept on racism. I was learning quickly that my childhood in Wolfville was not typical for Black Nova Scotians.

In the newsroom, I heard about a seventeen-acre "slum" in downtown Halifax. In 1957, all three levels of government and the Canada Mortgage and Housing Corporation decided which areas of the city most needed repairs. Planner and urban designer Gordon Stephenson had been commissioned by the City of Halifax in the previous year to prepare an urban renewal plan. The Gordon Stephenson report found dozens of houses and old commercial buildings that should have been condemned years ago, as they were rundown, without hot water, and infested with rats and filth. The report blamed years of neglect by landlords. Many of the large families who lived in the houses were Black.

Often, a grandmother, mother, father, and ten children would live in three rooms, plus a kitchen. They'd share a bathroom with nine other families. Tuberculosis was common. So was alcoholism. Kids often skipped school. Many fathers worked long, hard hours to pay the rent and other bills. Some of the children lived four to a room and didn't have hot water. The cramped, uncomfortable houses drove many people out onto the streets in the evening, seeking a sense of freedom and a breath of fresh air.

We really needed more Black journalists, reporters, feature writers, and photographers to tell their stories, but they were few and far between in the late 1950s. It was unnerving to walk through that community, because it wasn't just poor Blacks who lived there, but dangerous white criminals, bootleggers, and pimps who all worked their businesses out of the seventeen acres. I didn't know anyone who lived there, and I didn't understand the culture. Most Nova Scotians never read about the conditions, and there was no public outcry about those conditions. Instead, attention focused on the petty criminals, some of whom would break into a store simply to get enough money for food or more booze; these were some of the poorest people in the province.

Wealthy slum landlords would collect cash each week from the ten to fifteen tenants in each house, but they spent little of that income on rodent or insect extermination, proper heating, plumbing, or new roofs and flooring. The landlords were mostly white and lived in the prosperous South End of Halifax. The houses were worth nothing, but the landlords used them as cash cows. I felt inadequate when I realized that these buildings were home to hundreds of Black people who lived an excruciatingly uncomfortable existence, and I knew their stories needed to be told. Ultimately the seventeen-acre community was taken over by several of Nova Scotia's leading entrepreneurs. They demolished it and built Scotia Square, a shopping mall and office complex.

As a cub reporter, I enjoyed being around journalists. Their "nose for news" inspired me. They were inquisitive. The good ones wanted to probe and ask more questions to get to the root of an issue. It amazed me to see them sniffing out a story, and then following it beyond where they could have guessed it would lead. It was a great learning experience for me.

As a university student, I continued to report for the *Herald* on a part-time basis over the next five years; I was a stringer who covered Acadia and the Valley from Wolfville. I later worked as a news editor with CBC Television and Radio in Winnipeg and Halifax. At CBC I had my baptism into the politics of trade unions. Indeed, I became a member of the American Newspaper Guild. There were strict rules about what sort of work you could do under your union contract. That meant I was stuck as a news editor, which was not particularly exciting or creative. I would collect a story from one of our newswire sources and rewrite it with CBC language, using CBC-approved words and phrases. We then handed the words to the announcer—who belonged to another union—and they would read them on-air.

I had tried writing a novel and some poetry and essays, but the big bright light never came on. Interestingly enough, I had written a play called *An Inquiry into Modern Poetry*, filled with characters I had created who read from the original poems of Richard Wright, James Baldwin, Maya Angelou, and T. S. Eliot. It played on a few different shows on student radio and proved quite popular and provocative. The writing bug stayed with me all my life. Throughout my career, I wrote dozens of editorials, op-ed pieces, and other feature columns for various periodicals, journals, and newspapers. But I knew that writing was not going to be the way that I would put food on the table. My favourite poet was Maya Angelou, whose poetry seems to sing and dance off the page. My accomplished cousin, George Elliott Clarke, who clearly understood the ethic of the Nova Scotia Black man, has a never-ending talent for producing wonderful prose and poetry. These poets all could make difficult concepts seem so clear. But, as I noted, writing was not my main passion.

❧

But what *was* my passion? My older half-brother, William Oliver, took a degree in divinity and preached the word of the Lord, but he also was a visionary about the needs of his people and had components of social work, politics, and social activism in his ministry. He was always looking for ways to improve the standard of living for Blacks throughout the province. In 1945, he founded the Nova Scotia Association for the Advancement of Coloured People (NSAACP) at the Cornwallis Street Baptist Church in Halifax's North End. The NSAACP established fifty-six branches in communities throughout the province. My brother also started the Black United Front and worked with Premier Robert Stanfield to create the Nova Scotia Human Rights Commission in 1967. He was a powerful mentor and source of inspiration.

Mr. Stanfield was a Renaissance man. Born into a successful textile manufacturing business family in Truro, NS, the hub of the province, he studied law at Harvard Law School, where he excelled. He retained a lifelong interest in education. He became premier of Nova Scotia in 1956, the year I graduated from high school. Stanfield assigned himself the education portfolio, and he had a personal desire to do something about the dismal plight of Black and Indigenous people in Nova Scotia. The poorest people he knew near his home in Truro were, as he put it, "Negro people."

While he was premier, I was truly blessed to have had countless opportunities to interface with him about the Black community. I first met him when I was student chairman of the campus history club at Acadia University. I invited him to be a guest speaker at one of our meetings. After his speech, we students had a chance to meet him. For me, it was the beginning of a wonderful mentorship and friendship with Mr. Stanfield that lasted for decades.

During one of our private lunches, he asked me why there were not more Black tennis players like Arthur Ashe emerging from Nova Scotia. He was clearly interested in finding ways to promote our Black heroes, and he loved sports. I took it as my opening to talk about where he should start in combating systemic racism in our province. Arthur Ashe was born and raised in Richmond, Virginia, very near where my grandfather's family had been held as slaves. Ashe's father worked as a caretaker for a park with pools and tennis courts, and that's how Ashe got his start. In Nova Scotia, you'd struggle to find a tennis court anywhere near the inner city. Success in tennis would indeed have raised the profile of Blacks in the province, but we had even more fundamental problems to fix first.

Stanfield resigned as premier and MLA in 1967 and ran for a seat in the federal Parliament. I ran his campaign for the Progressive Conservative Party, and he won handsomely. He was soon elected leader of the party.

One day, years later, after he had retired from politics completely, I received a call to have lunch with him at the Halifax Club. Stanfield and I took a corner table where we could talk privately. He was taller than I was, and quite gaunt. He walked slowly. He ate slowly. He spoke even more slowly—so slowly in fact that I often wanted to finish his sentences for him. Behind all of that was the steely, disciplined, brilliant A-plus Harvard mind of a man who, as premier, had led our province with progressive laws and policies that sparked and drove our economy and attracted significant business investment to all parts of the province.

He ordered fresh pan-fried haddock and tea. He loved haddock. I knew that because I had hosted many private dinner parties for him at my home where I had been head chef. On one occasion, I served a delightful baked stuffed haddock with a summer savory sauce, and he and his wife really enjoyed it. After the staff brought his tea, he asked for some hot water. As the pot with the tea leaves would start to darken in colour, he would add a little hot water from the other canister to dilute it and make it nice and hot again.

He had an incredible sense of humour and his dry wit often caused people to burst into laughter. Sometimes I would have to turn my head so no one would see me laughing. He was great fun to be around. Sometimes I would get little two- or three-line notes from him with ticklingly funny endings. But today's luncheon was not the day for humour. Mr. Stanfield said to me that while he was premier he took note of the deplorable way Blacks and Indigenous people were treated and he deeply regretted that he had done nothing about it at the time. He said it was time something was done about it.

"I am retired now. I have the time and the determination to do something about it," he said. "What do you think I can do to help?"

My mind flashed to the deplorable housing in so many of our communities, and the shortage of good teachers and the lack of education infrastructures in our communities. I thought about money for more bursaries and scholarships so more Black youth could obtain a university education. At our lunch, I suggested we should begin by engaging and learning from the larger Black community in Nova Scotia. That subsequently led to many meetings with the leaders of the largest Black organizations in the province.

We began by meeting at my five-bedroom house in central Halifax. It was a convenient and comfortable place to have a meeting. At the first gathering of our ad hoc group we put many thoughts on the table, such as support for daycare, making adult education more accessible to parents in the community, giving more legal support and assistance to our youth in conflict with the law, and finding ways to win employment opportunities for our teenagers.

On the second meeting a couple of weeks later, we discussed implementation of these ideas and tried to prioritize them. At a third meeting, Mr. Stanfield told us he had been listening and wanted to propose that he get in touch with some of his friends who ran the largest companies in the province to see about starting a Black internship program with mentoring support for our youth. At the fourth meeting, where we were to settle on the specific details of the plan, only Mr. Stanfield and I showed up. I tried to phone the community leaders who were members of our group, but I could reach no one. Mr. Stanfield outlined to me who he had phoned and what successes he'd had, and I told him I would send him a note on what had happened to our meeting when I found out. That night, subject to the approval of the other leaders, we settled on the idea of an internship program for Black youth at the telephone company, which was a very large organization, as a start.

In the past, our fragmented, under-educated, poverty-ridden Black communities had been characterized as being "like crabs in a barrel." When one crab reaches the top, ready to climb out and make its way, the others pull it back into the pit of poverty and the place of little hope.

Regrettably, that's what happened here. The tentacles of white privilege had extended into our communities and indoctrinated even our leaders with the belief that we were not worthy to organize such a big undertaking with a white man as prominent and influential as Mr. Stanfield. White privilege had even infiltrated the heart of our biggest and most influential Black organizations and its leaders. Like the allegorical crabs in a barrel, our Black leaders had had a meeting without me and asked: "Why do we have to meet in Don Oliver's house?" Another asked, "Who appointed Don to be the chairman of the meetings?" They said I was not the leader of any of our Black organizations, so why should I even be involved? The evils of generations of suppression and degradation just came pouring out over the good intentions of a white man—a white man who could have made a major difference by tempering white privilege and providing Black people with the opportunity to take their places as equal and proud citizens in Canada.

So that was the end of the Stanfield meetings with the Black community, but the internship/apprentice program did get set up at the telephone company and it became a success.

These are important lessons our leaders must understand even today. We must support one another. I recall that in a speech, Stokely Carmichael—a brilliant thinker and a prominent organizer in the civil rights movement in the US, who once stayed just blocks from where I lived in Halifax—said that racist assumptions of white superiority have been so deeply ingrained into the fibre of society that they affect the entire functioning of the national subconscious. That includes the subconscious of our Black leaders.

Later, Mr. Stanfield was approached by a foundation on whose board he had sat for years. They wanted to give him a gift as thanks for his service. He and his wife came to see me about what to do with the money—$50,000—and we discussed various types of education vehicles to help the community. As a result, he established the Right Honourable Robert L. Stanfield Bursary Fund at Dalhousie University, which was reserved for Black students from Nova Scotia.

❖

But back when all of that was still in the future, my father was strongly encouraging me to follow the divinity route, while I secretly thought I had an interest or inclination toward academia and diplomacy. I began my studies at Acadia University in a quandary about what I would do with my life. As soon as I was registered, I had the opportunity to look for a job to help pay for the rest of the school year. Good fortune landed me a job on my second day on campus, working in the registration department as a typist. The job: to type up application forms, bursaries, and other documents. Later I got a job restocking books at the library. I often struggled to return interesting books and periodicals to the shelves; colleagues would often find me in a corner, sitting on the floor, book in hand, lost in some new subject. I worked in the dining hall serving plated meals to tables of ten. I loved it. The hall was as noisy as a stadium during a football game, with hundreds of students talking, teasing, and clanging their bowls and plates.

I earned a lot of money as a jazz musician, playing the trumpet at dances on weekends and for other special events. Those long hours practising after high school were finally paying off! I played a cornet solo at a music festival and once won first prize for my rendition of Handel's Largo. My mother's excellence in music had instilled itself in all her children.

I loved music and once hitchhiked from Nova Scotia to Stratford, Ontario, just to hear the celebrated Canadian pianist Glenn Gould perform at the Stratford Theatre. My own musical talents were put into perspective by the brilliant Austrian organist at our Baptist church in Wolfville. Eugen Gmeiner had immigrated to Canada in 1956, the same year I graduated high school and started university. Gmeiner had studied in Europe and the US and was celebrated for his interpretations of Bach. He and I became great friends. I would sometimes turn the pages for him when he gave a Bach recital. That created some scary moments. I worried I would turn the page too quickly, or too slowly, even by a few seconds, which could ruin the performance. But if I did it right, I got to sit for hours and listen to him play.

His feet and hands and that huge Casavant Brothers Opus 1950 organ could elicit a state of enchantment in his listeners. The organ had 1,287 pipes, 3 divisions, 2 manuals, and 23 stops, and Gmeiner knew how to use them all. He often wandered off the page during our church services and followed the spirit into what one listener called an "ecstasy of improvisational genius." It warmed my soul when we played at Christmas, he on the giant organ on the floor, I up in the balcony with my trumpet. We played a duet of Christmas carols that echoed off the high ceiling. Our performance, filled with some interesting harmonies, was very well received.

I had an extraordinary experience during the summer of 1958 that helped shape the man I would become. I went to Toronto for the fifth Baptist Youth World Conference. We heard from Canada's new prime minister, John Diefenbaker, who was also a devout Baptist. Diefenbaker's Progressive Conservative government would soon create the Canadian Bill of Rights, our country's first federal law protecting fundamental human rights and freedoms. I listened carefully to our prime minister's talk and he became a great influence on my social and political thinking.

But the star of the event was Rev. Martin Luther King Jr. He was the most famous Black man in North America—maybe in the whole world. All eyes locked on him as he began to speak. I sat high in the rafters, far from him, but soon felt like I was sitting at his feet. I felt like I was in church on Sunday, listening to a passionate, hour-long sermon. King told us about his search for meaning in slavery and the most Christ-like way to escape oppression. "What is the path to freedom?" he asked us. Some tried the constitution and the courts, he said, but those failed them. Black people in the American south—the home of my enslaved ancestors—had been held for centuries in subjugation and had no organization, apart from the church. The enslaved people were untrained for any kind of physical combat, were unarmed, and were disunited, he said, "and, most importantly, psychologically and morally unprepared for the deliberate spilling of blood."

King saw this as a strength. From those pieces he built his doctrine of non-violent resistance. This path did not seek revenge, but instead called on Black people to champion change. Tremendous applause and numerous standing ovations burst out like fireworks throughout his speech. He moved us so powerfully that we had to react, had to show him we heard. He preached freedom, equality, justice, and love. The big roaring crowd, the noise, the passion, and the talk of freedom gave us hope for a better future.

❖

Early on at Acadia University I took a course called History 1, taught by a Professor Wilson—a person so eloquent he made eighteenth-century European history come to life. We had our first test after Thanksgiving. Afterward, Professor Wilson told our class of about a hundred students how disappointed he was with the test results, which he had spent hours reading and marking. Then he said that one paper had stood out. He said he wanted to read it aloud as an example of a good paper, and the way test and exam papers should be written. I recognized the words immediately, but couldn't quite believe my ears. When he was done, he said the paper had been written by Don Oliver, who had earned a 92—the top grade in the class.

I was in a state of shock. This day changed my life, because up until that moment I had no idea if I'd written a good paper or a bad one. I spent much of my day serving meals to other students at the dining hall or shelving books in the library. And now I learned I was an excellent student. The two things seemed oxymoronic.

Some students started calling me "the brain" and engineering students came to me asking for help writing their papers. That experience in history class was transformative. I would never be the same. I had made some good marks before—I'd earned a 100 in geometry in grade ten—but this was different. I could no longer be the shy little child afraid to speak his name in kindergarten.

It was the first marked change from being a rudderless child to being a teen student maturing into manhood. It helped to give me the strength in later life to take on the challenges of systemic racism and other global problems. Part of my modesty was because I knew I wasn't the smartest kid in my family. My three sisters were exceptional students and "brainier" than me. Professor Wilson inspired me, challenged me, and made me realize some of my innate, latent strengths. It really was quite the day.

I worked my way busily through my four years at Acadia University, taking extra courses, playing trumpet in the jazz band on weekends, chairing several university organizations, in addition to working on the family farm. At the end, I felt just as uncertain about my life as I had at the start. But I must have looked more certain to other people, as I was surprised to learn in the 1960 student yearbook. The student council published my photo and name and what seemed like an impressive list of accomplishments, on campus and off.

"An intense student and a deep thinker, Don has made a marked contribution to student life at Acadia," it read. "You may see him interviewing professors and students on the latest topical issue and later, wreathed in smoke and thought, he may be seen in the *Athenaeum* office typing out his latest provocative editorial. With his sense of dedication and perceptive mind we are sure that Donnie will be highly successful in his chosen field of journalism." Clearly, I decided not to become a journalist, but I have continued to write and publish for sixty-five years.

Not even 1 percent of the students at Acadia were Black, including students from the West Indies. A number of those students were guests at our home for dinner. I made friends with students from different backgrounds, including, of course, lots of white people. I had many dates, but nothing serious. That was good for me. I was maturing but still did not know which paths I wanted to walk

Donald Oliver graduated from Acadia University in Wolfville, Nova Scotia, in 1960 with an honours bachelor of arts degree with a major in history and minors in English and philosophy. He was class valedictorian.

in life. The traditions and examples of my maternal and paternal grandparents and parents gave me guidance, but I still needed to grow up and learn. I loved Acadia's small campus, where I could talk to professors after class. I flourished on the hillside campus, and it was no surprise. I'd grown up on it, knew it intimately from working with my father, and now had made it my own home.

I graduated with an honours bachelor of arts degree with a major in history and minors in English and philosophy. I was class valedictorian. On convocation day I felt butterflies in my stomach as I walked onto the stage to give my address to a room full of students and professors.

"Today we stand before a changing, restless world," I told them. "As the cries of students in Asia, Africa, and Latin America become blatant to our ears with their craving for freedom, we cry back our thanks to Acadia. We cherish even the minute aspects of liberty and freedom that have been placed before us for our personal disposal during the last four years....We need hardly say that since our thirst for freedom is insatiable, it has not been quenched; yet, we have tasted enough to want to defend it."

I graduated in 1960, and like many students my age, had no idea what to do next. I had studied John Wesley's teaching for my history honours thesis and found it intellectually stimulating. His ideas made a considerable contribution to my future social and political thinking. My thesis was called "Wesleyanism as a Vehicle of Social and Political Criticism in the Century Before 1848." In that period in Germany and France, great upheavals changed the world. John Wesley's teaching and preaching influenced the social and political arena throughout England such that they did not have revolutions or social upheavals. My research, and the background readings I did, provided the opportunity for me to think more deeply about the dignity of work and equality as I also studied the epoch-changing work of William Wilberforce and the slave trade.

I was really starting to love academic life. I've mentioned that my father would have preferred that I enter divinity school and become a Baptist preacher as his first son had. Reverend Oliver had had an outstanding career as a preacher, human rights activist, and adult education advocate, particularly in the Black communities sprinkled throughout Nova Scotia. I was very interested in pursuing an academic career and becoming a professor in philosophy, particularly existentialism (which I loved), or history. Diplomacy was always in the back of my mind.

All aptitude tests told me that, fundamentally, I wanted to help and serve people. I saw an advertisement for a big scholarship to Dalhousie Law School and I thought I should apply. Perhaps I could graduate and find ways for the justice system to help to solve some problems in society, and at the same time, serve my community. I spent a year praying, thinking, and researching to help me decide which road I should take.

During my year of searching and pondering, I had also applied for a Rhodes scholarship to Oxford University. I felt I had the sports and scholastic achievements, a strong interest in helping others, and my personal integrity, so I applied. I got an interview. I put on my best suit, polished my shoes, and tried to make myself as presentable as I could. I made my way to downtown Halifax and the historic Halifax Club—an exclusive, elegant, private social club for the business and political leaders of the province. Years later I would meet Mr. Stanfield for lunch inside, but in 1960, it was a whole new experience for me. Entering the stylish Victorian building for the interview was the first time I'd ever stepped inside. I looked up at the high ceilings and the stairway to the second floor, seeing the magnificent mahogany furniture in the side rooms, the ornamental rugs, and the large leather sofas. A doorman—or perhaps he was a butler—greeted me and showed me where to hang my coat. He took me to a sitting room, where I awaited an invitation to the interview itself. I was, to say the least, a little awestruck by the club.

It seemed like an eternity before I was finally called into a room and introduced to the interviewers, who were representative, it seemed, of the highest offices in the province, including the chief justice of the Supreme Court of Nova Scotia. After polite introductory comments, the discussion turned on several principal questions, one of which was on current affairs, which I was able to address appropriately.

"We note you have taken some philosophy courses and you have achieved some excellent grades," they asked. "In the eighteenth century, Immanuel Kant was an important thinker. Can you explain to us his categorical imperative?"

I may have smiled to myself. I knew and understood the moral theory extremely well. I had been studying it in various classes over the last two years. I was able to answer in great detail, explaining that the first formulation was what Kant called universality, which he believed was our duty to act in such a manner that we would want everyone else to act in a similar manner in similar circumstances toward others. Warming up, I told them how Kant argued we should act at all times as though it were a universal law. I explained the difference between a categorical and a hypothetical imperative.

When I was done, I quietly took a deep breath. I was feeling pleased with how things were proceeding. They did not ask any questions based on my response to that question. When all their other questions had been asked and answered, the chair of the panel told me that, before I'd arrived in the room for the interview, the panel had held a private meeting in which they'd discussed my application and decided they had to ask me one extra question. I nodded and waited for them to speak.

"How do you think Nova Scotians would feel being represented at Oxford by a Negro person?" he asked.

Wow! I hadn't expected that. The sleeping bear of racism raised its head again. I paused for a moment to compose myself. I carefully gave them a thoughtful response I hoped would reassure them I was a good candidate. I told them I had always worked hard and would continue to work hard at Oxford. I told them I was a proud Canadian and intended to return from England to devote the rest of my life to making Canada a better country. I told them that the colour of my skin, or "being a Negro person," would not be a barrier to my passionately pursuing those goals.

"Thank you," they said.

The interview was over. I left the room and collected my coat. Six months later, the panel chair wrote me a letter saying I had done well and strongly encouraged me to try again next year. I did not. I turned their last question over in my mind for decades. What I heard them really asking was: "Because there is white privilege in Nova Scotia, shouldn't a white boy get this scholarship and not a Negro boy?" And, "Do you think the people of Nova Scotia are prepared to see a Negro boy receive such a prestigious award?"

In other words, I concluded they thought most Nova Scotians might be upset with the panel itself if a Negro boy won such a prestigious honour. Surely they had to ask themselves as a panel, how would that affect their status in society?

I did win one of Dalhousie Law School's five coveted Sir James Dunn scholarships. I accepted it and resolved the question of my career path. I would become a lawyer to fight racism in Canada. But I had one more journey before my future became law.

Chapter Four

AFRICA

THERE WAS SOMETHING SPECIAL IN THE AIR. THE MORNING
was sunny with a clear blue sky. The air was humid, but we felt
cooled by a nice gentle breeze. The fragrance of summer roses was
evident and the scent seemed to have a special freshness, a new-
ness, like we expect from a newly planted garden. In fact, it was
the first time these trees and flowers had filled the area with their
kaleidoscope of brilliant colours—a magical sight and, for me, a
transformational moment. Even the green grass of the carefully
manicured lawn seemed ready for something special. The scent
of roses and all the other floral charm had a calming effect that
camouflaged what was about to unfold in the White House's Rose
Garden.

It was June 1962, and we had been in Washington for a week of
intensive orientation sessions and briefings before departing abroad.
It's normally hot and steamy in Washington near the end of June,
and this week had been no exception.

We were a small group of university students from the United
States and Canada, lined up outside the White House, about to

receive a short briefing by Rev. James Robinson, a highly respected Black preacher and social activist, and a friend of President John F. Kennedy. He told us that the president of the United States had invited us to the Rose Garden outside the Oval Office to greet us and wish us well before we boarded our planes for our trip abroad with Operation Crossroads Africa—the brainchild of Reverend Robinson. We were escorted onto the grounds and had a few minutes to be awestruck by the natural beauty of the garden before the arrival of the president.

Suddenly, as though from nowhere, JFK appeared with his security detail, who kept their distance. He welcomed us warmly with his clearly recognizable New England accent. He was a lot shorter than I thought he would be, but he certainly had a Hollywood aura about him. He was warm and exuded confidence and charm, and instantly had us in the palm of his hand. In his remarks, which it seems I shall never forget, he said he had been impressed for some years by the work Reverend Robinson was doing in sending students to Africa to promote world peace and friendship, and to promote mutual understanding with the people in the African countries where they worked.

The president told us that students who had participated in Operation Crossroads Africa were "really the progenitors of the Peace Corps." He said the work we did as volunteers—building schools, teaching students, helping with agricultural and irrigation projects—was what inspired him to move ahead with the legislation required by congress to make his dream a reality. It was really quite a moment, and I stood there absorbing it all as a twenty-three-year-old law student. My going to Africa on a Crossroads project suddenly became something very special. I did not get to shake his hand, but I got a photo of him with the Rose Garden in the background from about eight feet away. A thrilling moment, and one I've never forgotten.

Thoroughly excited and jazzed up after hearing the words of encouragement from the president, our group left for our hotel for one more medical debriefing before we headed to the airport and off for the long flight to Africa. We were Ethiopia-bound. Operation Crossroads scouts had gone to an area of enormous need in the north, called Tigray province. The area had been hit by a devastating drought that had killed off most of the parents and the elderly, leaving only a few children to fend very much for themselves. There was a small school, but it needed an extension and extensive interior repair. We were to base ourselves at a small village called Maimisham.

The long flight was exhausting, but I couldn't sleep. As we approached Addis Ababa, the capital city, we were all wide awake, with great anticipation. After all, Ethiopia is the cradle of human civilization. We could see the lights of the airport clearly, and as the sun broke through the early morning, some areas below lit up, showing a fairly large city. As our plane approached the airport, I could sense that the pent-up excitement would explode into strong applause for the pilots as soon as the wheels touched the tarmac. Looking out my window, after wheels-down, I saw a couple of massive billboards, one promoting a Hollywood film starring Elvis Presley. There he was, larger than life, looking like he was going to step out and join us on the runway. The second, equally large, billboard was for Coca-Cola, which is headquartered in Atlanta. From Atlanta to Addis Ababa. This wasn't the sort of culture shock I was expecting.

The tires came to a screeching halt on the runway. I had arrived at my ancestral home; the very place where humankind began. I looked forward to seeing real, natural African culture from a people who had kept their country for thousands of years and had never been assimilated. Ethiopia is one of the oldest countries in the world and was developed around 980 BC. Many traditional customs remained untarnished because there were no major invasions. We arrived early in the morning, and as we drove through the streets we could see people dressed in long white cotton shammas, talking, laughing, and enjoying life as they walked holding hands.

We were being taken to Haile Selassie University in the heart of the town, where we would stay and have a further orientation for another week. As we walked up the stairs to what was the student cafeteria, many students gathered around and began some great conversations. They spoke in wonderful English and were happy to see us. It wasn't long before I tasted my first cup of that famous Ethiopian coffee. It was black and strong and certainly needed some sugar, but it was wonderfully flavourful and tasted like nothing I had ever had before. It was delicious.

After we had some pieces of gray unleavened bread called injera to go with the coffee, the jet lag set in. We were shown to our individual rooms in the student residence, where after a wonderful hot shower I slept for five hours. I had to be ready for lectures that afternoon and evening on such things as medical precautions, footwear, clothing, and wildlife in the area where we were going, and then for another briefing on the current government.

As I went to my first orientation session, I noticed that a number of local students came around in a very calm, friendly way, anxious to learn who we foreigners were, where we were from, and what we would be doing. I was as interested to learn about them and their ancient country, which had the largest population of any landlocked country in the world. I was struck by how calm, quiet, and almost easy going the students were in general. They were very hospitable, in the sense that they made us feel welcome, and their kindness shone through in virtually everything they did.

Addis was a busy city with lots of commerce, and the streets were packed with people coming and going, selling various wares as they went. But we spent a lot of time in the classroom learning about governments and the customs and language of the people in the place where we had been assigned. Haile Selassie, whose official title was "the Conquering Lion of Judah," was the emperor. Our orientation sessions were at the Haile Selassie University on Haile Selassie Avenue, near the Haile Selassie Theatre. He had several massive palaces throughout the country, and when his entourage would pass through some of the rural areas, the locals were ordered to bow. He was a force without equal. He had a commanding presence in the country.

Many local students joined us for dinner that night for more conversation—and we had so many questions for them. In many ways interacting with the students was the best part of the week-long orientation. There were, of course, a number of very serious and important things we needed to know and understand about water, diseases, religious customs, local customs, security, and personal health.

The week passed quickly. We were told to pack our bags, including the sleeping bags and pillows we had brought from home, and get ready for an early morning departure by bus to drought-stricken Tigray province. Before leaving Canada, I had read that Ethiopia had only twenty-eight miles of paved road in the entire country of more than sixty million people, and that those roads had been built by the Italians during their short occupation after Mussolini invaded in 1935.

We did not get far away from downtown Addis before the beautiful Italian paved roads ended. Looking out the bus window, I was conscious that we saw very little evidence of poverty or substandard housing. We did see the impressive new Africa Hall, home for the United Nations in Africa. I made a mental note to investigate, and when I returned to Canada I learned that the emperor had built tall fences along the route to Africa Hall so visiting dignitaries would not see the tin shacks and poverty in which many Ethiopians lived.

Donald Oliver is shown here holding a soda bottle (possibly Coca-Cola) during his trip to Ethiopia in 1962 with Operation Crossroads Africa. At left is an Ethiopian student named Emanuel; the other two young men are American students who were also OCA participants.

We drove north over the mountains through rough, rocky, narrow dirt roads. We drove up and around, and through sharp turns in the mountain on such scary terrain that I was afraid to look out the window. The brakes were loud and noisy and, frankly, didn't seem to work that well. There were many occasions during that multi-day trip where we could have gone over the side at any time and there would have been no chance of a happy ending. There were also many times our bus driver seemed to think he was in the Indy 500, because he simply drove too fast for the conditions.

Looking out the window, I was fascinated by the terraces, Ethiopia's ancient system of soil water management. We passed thousands of them in the mountains. I knew some farmers grew coffee and produced honey from their bees, but I learned they also produced vegetables and livestock. I studied how the mud and soil had been pulled up to form those beautiful terraces in order to prevent all the rainwater from careening down the mountainside. These small, private farmers lived from harvest to harvest, making them vulnerable to famine in bad years.

We finally reached the small village of Maimisham, where we were to spend the summer. We had left the mountains and arrived on a flat plateau. It would be hard to call it a community. My western eyes noticed the lack of a corner store or drugstore, or even a dentist's or a doctor's office. No roads, either, and no cars. It did have a loose collection of round, thatched-roof huts, and some camels and goats. Most of the cattle, goats, and camels that had sustained the lives of nomadic groups in the region had perished from lack of food. I learned that many of the cows were tubercular. Many people in that area were nomads. We were shown to our huts and we put down ground sheets and our sleeping bags. Then we went to see what remained of the school we were to build an extension to.

Grief hung in the air. Just a few years before we arrived, a devastating drought had hit from 1958 to 1960. In the Tigray province a hundred thousand people had died. The shallow soil struggled to produce food in good times, and after back-to-back "rain seasons" without any rain, grain crops like teff and sorghum simply dried up. Virtually all the parents and grandparents had starved to death. We were there to help build a bigger school for the surviving children.

The walls were to be made of stones and rocks. We had no cement or ready-mix to support them, so our group took the job of carrying rocks and stones to the school. We also scavenged for sticks to use as window casings. We got to work. Morning after morning, week after week, I worked on a chain gang passing rocks along. I glanced at each rock, worried I'd see the dangerous black scorpions that often clung to them. On the surface, it was identical to the work I'd done in my summer construction job. Emotionally, it was totally different. It wasn't about me and a paycheque—I wasn't even getting paid! At least, not in money.

Our leader selected the rocks and built the walls. He used a mixture of straw, mud, and water called chika to hold them together. In the afternoons, we taught the students. We also travelled through the community, meeting with locals and learning about their daily struggles. We helped out when we could. Everyone was so gentle, soft-spoken, and kind. Many did not speak English.

Our group decided to communicate using the universal language of food. We would roast a couple of goats and host a local feast. We dug a pit, gathered wood, and built a pile to cook the feast. While we did that, the rest of our group sourced the goats and prepared them for cooking. We laid logs, set the fire, and put the goat meat on grates. The scent of the cooking meat put everyone in a good mood. We feasted together; the food was plentiful and delicious.

We had brought a new Polaroid camera from America. Even we were amazed at how you could point, shoot, and then look at the photo. No need to wait for it to get developed! We went for a walk with it one day and asked a local man if we could take his photo. He agreed. We pointed and clicked. The camera started buzzing and soon a crowd gathered. We all watched, amazed, as it pushed out a white piece of paper with the image developing on it. We shook it dry and showed him the photo of himself. He was surprised and delighted. Some of the people had never seen their own faces before, other than as an image reflected in a pool of water.

One local who spoke a bit of English told us they had never seen a white person before. In our group of six, five were white; I was the only Black person. For a change, it wasn't my skin that caught people's attention and changed their behaviour. When they saw white people, the Ethiopians covered their mouths with their hands and turned their heads to try and hide their giggles. It seemed a mix of nervousness and respect. White people were clearly a strange sight to them and they tried not to stare.

For me, the Ethiopia trip was a break from the racism that dominated so much of life in Canada. Our group got along well, and we all got along well with the locals. Leave it to Africa to be the place where diversity, tolerance, and respect just seemed the natural response. Locals expected people to be and look different. Ethnic diversity was a simple fact.

It was all a little difficult for me. I was perplexed and really in a quandary. I was thousands of miles from home, with my feet firmly planted on Mother Earth—at home in Africa, with my people. I felt strange, as if the waters I'd always swum in had changed. I didn't feel superior to my white colleagues. I didn't feel inferior. We were just the same—humans trying to help other humans. As I adjusted, I enjoyed the wonderful sense of purity, almost naivety, about racism.

I certainly had a lot of time to reflect on it, as our huts had no electricity, no telephones, no showers, no sinks, no toilets, and no running water. We did have two candles, but they were only for emergencies. When the sun set, it was dark and we went to bed. When the sun rose, it was light and we woke and worked. We followed the sun. We soon learned to avoid nighttime bathroom use, as that meant leaving the safety of the hut and entering the great darkness of full night, finding a spot away from the settlement, and squatting, ears perked up for the howls of hyenas. We sometimes heard them growling and screaming and drawing closer, but fortunately they never attacked.

Finally, after much work, we stepped back and looked at the completed school expansion. It really looked nice and appeared to be ready to last a long time. I felt a tear fall from my eye and hit my cheek.

The people were so warm, kind, and welcoming. In Africa, North American life seemed so cold and distant. At home, kindness wasn't our default attitude toward strangers; instead we often felt a harsh distrust. On our last evening in the hut, we went around the space and asked each other what we would first order when we were back in North America. Hershey bars, steaks, beer, and a long hot bath topped the list.

We flew first to Nairobi for a stop in Kenya and were handed certificates commemorating our equator-crossing on the way. We were to spend a week debriefing at an Anglican mission in Limuru, just north of Nairobi. We drove through the stunning highlands and were awestruck at the scenic landscapes, beautiful farms, and plantations. It was all so peaceful and relaxing. We were warmly welcomed by the mission staff and shown to our individual rooms. As we were debriefed, I noticed a lot of flies and ants, but said to myself—this is just life in Africa.

I went to my room and sat at my desk to catch up on my letter writing. I suddenly felt something on my legs. Then I saw things moving in my pants. A scream rose up from a nearby room. I looked at the floor and felt a gut-punch of horror when I saw thousands of red-looking ants. They were swarming through the complex. I pulled them off me, but their numbers were overwhelming. I tore off my clothes and dashed to the shower, my heart pounding. Could this be it? Were these bugs deadly? Was I about to die? I calmed down and told myself I'd already been bitten many times and I wasn't dead yet. I looked at the stings on my body and saw no evidence of welts. My heart slowed. I lathered up well with soap. In the hall, I could hear the staff going room to room, telling everyone the ants were harmless. They sprayed the ants with what looked like vinegar and water and cleaned our rooms. I felt a great relief. And the hot shower felt amazing.

While we were in Limuru, I went sightseeing one day, taking in the huge tea and coffee plantations that had been built by English colonists. We stopped at Kiambethu Tea Farm, an historic colonial tea plantation with indigenous forests. As we drove up a dirt hill, we saw six barefoot Kenyans hard at work. They weren't picking tea, but pushing a black Jaguar sports car! The owner, a well-dressed English gentleman, walked slowly beside them. He had run out of gas.

I wondered—was this anti-Black racism, or old-fashioned colonialism? It reminded me that I wasn't home, but I would soon return to North America, where again my minority skin would matter. There would be the latent, all-pervasive white privilege with all its perks, and I would once again face the reality of the rising civil rights movement, and the physical and mental strife that came with it.

I would return to Canada, but I would forever keep a piece of Africa in my heart.

Chapter Five

THE LAW

THERE WERE MORE THAN A COUPLE OF TIMES IN MY LIFE when I forgot that my skin colour signalled an immediate physical and emotional problem for many white people in society. One day while I was at Dalhousie Law School, I was out walking with Darrel T. Warren, a fellow Sir James Dunn Scholar, a tall, six-foot, four-inch white man from Saskatchewan. Darrel, or Del as we called him, was passionate and very intense about everything he did. He and his wife had entertained me at their apartment for dinner a couple of times. She was very nice; a short woman with a winning smile. She made me feel comfortable and welcome in her home. I think they both wanted to learn more about eastern Canada and more about Black people. I sensed they had little direct experience with Blacks.

Del and I skipped an afternoon of studying one day in first year to go play pool. The pool game would be another way of feeling each other out to see just what type of game each of us had, and to learn even more about the person himself. He was eager and ready for the challenge and so was I. I didn't tell him that when I was in my mid-teens, onlookers would pay me twenty-five cents if I could break the balls and shoot all fifteen off without missing. I collected a lot of quarters that way.

We checked the Yellow Pages and found a pool hall near campus called the Cue and Cushion. We walked into the small hall in downtown Halifax and looked over its few tables. The room was dark and smelled of cigarette smoke. No music played. Hardly anyone was there. We walked to an open table, took down our cue sticks, racked the balls, and began to play. I got off to a great start and was on a nice run when Del vanished for a few moments. He returned limping. I looked at him with concern and surprise. What had happened to him? He was very agitated and anxious. He said to me in a stern voice, "Leave your cue stick on the table and come with me outdoors immediately."

I did what he said and followed him as he limped out the front door. We ran into a tall, skinny man with a big frown on his face so deep I could almost hear it. He had a cigarette draping from his lips. I sensed he was the manager or owner. He stared at me, dark and foreboding, and said: "Don't you realize you're Black? You can't come in here." He pointed his finger at Del. "You can stay." Then he pointed back at me. "You have to go." His racism was right in my face.

How could I ever forget something so blatant and fundamental—that I was Black in a world where that meant I would be treated worse than white people, no matter what. This pool hall manager had the white power and privilege to remind me he thought I was not equal to white people. That "he could stay but I must go," merely because of the colour of my skin. There was no sign on the door saying I could not go into the hall to play. I had not lived long away from the safety of my family home in Wolfville and this was a sharp reminder that I would always have to be ready to defend my human rights at all times. This billiard hall experience instilled in me that I will be living virtually all my life with a constant reminder that I am different from most other Canadians, and that somehow I must prove that I am worthy to enjoy the same benefits as the white majority.

Del and I walked back to campus, thoughtful under the afternoon light. I asked him why he was limping. He stopped. "I just made it up," he said. "I did not want to tell you the things the man said about you when he pulled me aside and told me that you had to go. I felt if I was limping you would not question it at all but would just follow me out, as you did."

Del did not want a scene inside the pool hall. I really think that Del was more shaken by the incident that I was. He had never been party to anything like that sort of blatant racism in his life. We five Oliver kids had been called "pickaninnies" in school, and we had seen a lot more than that. Back on campus, we started to talk about what had happened. Like good lawyers, we researched the issue. I called the Department of Justice in the provincial government and explained what had happened: my human rights had been violated on racial grounds. I said that such discrimination had to end. The person who took my call said legislation was being drafted that might help. They sent me a copy of the draft and requested my input. I made several notes for changes to the draft legislation. The bill, the Fair Accommodation Practices Act, would make it the law of the province that no one could be kept out of a place "to which the public was customarily admitted" on the basis of skin colour. The bill became a law, and later became part of a broader Human Rights Act. Places like the Cue and Cushion would no longer be legally allowed to bar the public based on race.

In the meantime, the Cue and Cushion would still have nothing to do with Black people in its establishment, so the owners had their lawyers incorporate them as a private society under the Societies Act.

You had to become a member of the society to enter the pool hall, and they could refuse membership to anyone. I never did apply to become a member!

❖

As I started my three years of law school, I was painfully aware of Africvillle. The well-established Black community on the shore of the Bedford Basin, which dated back at least as far as 1848, was only a few miles from the school. Halifax had decided it had to go and was demolishing it, home by home. Halifax City Council voted to remove the residents of the well-functioning community in 1964, the year I graduated. City Hall wanted the valuable land. The destruction of this Black community screamed off the front page of the newspapers. It had the momentum of a huge ocean liner that was too big to stop. And it couldn't be stopped. It rolled completely over Africville until there was nothing left: not a church, not a house, not a garden or a clothesline, and no deeds, birth records, school reports, or marriage or death certificates. Everything was gone. A whole community erased. The last house was demolished on January 2, 1970. Africville had been the billboard displaying so many of man's inhumanities to man. The city had shown deep disregard for the common decency and compassion that should be accorded all human beings just by virtue of their humanity. That respect had been lacking for decades with regard to Africville.

Throughout my youth, the Wolfville Olivers would sometimes take a Sunday drive to visit the Halifax Olivers at their Cornwallis Street Baptist Church. My stepbrother would preside. After church, we'd stay for a big, two-family dinner at the parsonage. During these visits, Reverend Oliver told us that Halifax wouldn't even send a road grader to fix Africville's huge potholes in the spring, nor would it send in a snowplow in the winter. The four hundred or so Black people who lived in Africville worked and paid taxes, but got no paved roads and no trash collection—though it did get the city dump. There was no city water or sewage system to Africville. Police and fire departments rarely protected Africville. My brother was clearly agitated, frustrated, and seeking answers—even from us. But what could he do? He was pleading and praying for some divine guidance to help stop the pillage of Africville, but he couldn't stop the destruction.

The *Chronicle Herald*, my old newspaper, reported that many residents had been promised $500 for their homes. It wrenched at my soul when I learned that some Black residents of Africville had received their payments in brown paper bags filled with nickels, dimes, and quarters, and perhaps the occasional fifty-cent piece. What a gross indignity! What a hateful, nasty—yes, appalling—way for one human being to treat another. It brought tears to my eyes. This tore my heart out. Such low-class behaviour was worse even than the systemic anti-Black racism it reflected. I wrote a strong letter of protest to the mayor. One academic researcher who was given access to all city documentation said I was the only Black Nova Scotian to file a protest with the city about the destruction of Africville.

Some things are hard to forget because they are so painful.

❖

So much depends on our human perceptions of others. Imagine, for a moment, that you have an appointment at an office with someone you have never met. The door opens and you see them for the first time. In that first instant, what is your impression—what do you see? What do you perceive? Do you see a blond woman who appears incredibly short? An elderly tall Black African man with a cane and a warm, cheerful smile? A very large, overweight man with a tweed jacket and a beard? A middle-aged man immaculately dressed in a silk suit and tie?

And what is the impression each of these people makes on you? Which would you likely be most comfortable with in a private conversation on the events of the day? What have you been programmed to see and believe about each of them? A lot of our views and opinions are developed by our sensory perceptions, which may change as we get closer to this individual, shake their hand, hear their voice, and observe the manner in which they express themselves. But blond hair, a beard, or a fancy silk suit will likely not leave as dominant a first impression as "Black African!" It just won't go away. You cannot hide it. The colour of my skin is a situational fact that has stayed with me for all my life. My pigmentation was not something I thought about every hour of every day. But, like a sleeping bear, it would awaken and raise its head on some of the most unexpected occasions, and I had to be ready.

I thought I might become a diplomat after graduating from law school at Dalhousie University. I didn't really know everything that diplomats did, but what I knew seemed interesting. I looked at the courses offered at the Fletcher School of International Law and Diplomacy, but I soon realized that working as a diplomat would mean working far away from Canada for long periods of time. Canada was home to my most personal experiences of racism and intolerance, and I had begun to think I could help make the business case for diversity in Canada. I decided not to go abroad to become a diplomat. I would be a diplomat in my own country, communicating not between nations, but between racial identities.

I didn't want to article for another year to be admitted to the bar, because I didn't then envision myself becoming a practicing lawyer. My friends and classmates persuaded me I should do the nine months to join a bar. Luckily, I got an offer to article at Stewart McKelvey Stirling Scales, Atlantic Canada's largest law firm, under well-known lawyer Donald Kerr. His admiralty expertise was legendary, and any shipwreck, salvage job, or dispute at sea on our side of the Atlantic Ocean would likely find its way to his desk. He also was a litigation lawyer, so I began to learn a lot about trial practice from him.

But then diplomacy came calling for me. Suddenly I heard from some excited academics who had a serious job offer for me in the newly independent East African nation of Tanganyika (later called Tanzania). I would be working in the country presided over by the revered leader Julius Nyerere, whom I had studied in history and knew as a pan-African statesman and liberator from British rule. Nyerere was a devout Catholic who wanted to improve the lives of the people he led. I was offered a position as the assistant dean of the law school in Dar es Salaam, the nation's capital at the time. Further, I would become dean the following year.

I must admit it appealed to me. Working in my motherland, Africa. Working with my own African people. Having a chance to work with Julius Nyerere. I had so recently given up on my idea of working as a diplomat and this seemed to satisfy that desire, too. I saw myself as dean of a leading African law school in a leading east coast African nation, speaking frankly about important matters of law and public policy with a leader as important as Nyerere. It started to sound like the opportunity of a lifetime. From Wolfville to Dar es Salaam.

I wore out my shoes pacing the floor, trying to decide if I should article in Halifax or become dean of a law school in Africa. I went to the senior partners in the law firm and put the African offer before them. They countered with how they saw the firm developing: they had openings for articling students now, and those students would likely become lawyers at the firm, but if I left for several years, that door could close permanently. There may be no openings on my return. I left the meeting undecided. I prayed, spoke with family and friends, and finally decided: I would stay in Canada. It was the same dilemma I'd faced over my interest in diplomacy. Whatever my life's work would be, it would be in Canada.

The bar society, the organization that regulated all lawyers in the province, arranged that each week a certain number of practicing lawyers would work at a legal aid clinic to give free legal advice, which included preparing documents and going to court with clients who needed help. In practice, the fifty-two most junior lawyers went twice a year to fulfill that obligation. Many of the intermediate lawyers in my firm had practices in taxation, receiverships, corporate mergers and acquisitions, and mechanic liens, and they didn't want to give up a good part of a week to do the legal aid pro bono work. I saw an opportunity: I'd do those weeks for them if they would undertake to give me some good legal files to work on in exchange. It was a great arrangement. I took on as many files and cases as I could and spent most mornings in court. Fascinated by the theatre of the law, I watched and learned from the best criminal lawyers in Nova Scotia as they addressed the court, dealt with clients, made timely objections, and raised and argued points of evidence and law. It complemented the academic case-study approach I'd learned in law school, as it was happening live in front of me. But unlike studying case law, in the courtroom no one knew how the cases would end.

In 1965, I was called to the Nova Scotia bar. Stewart McKelvey Stirling Scales made me an associate. But before I was assigned an office and things got under way, I was called in for a private meeting with one of the senior partners. He had conferred with the other three senior partners in the management group. He spoke to me frankly about how they felt my career would likely unfold. Reference was made to the four other lawyers joining the firm with me; all were very well known in the province and some had deep family business ties and personal connections with our bigger clients. Those connections and social networks, the senior partner explained to me, would be like an established conduit to bring new business to the firm and it meant their chances of promotion might be accelerated.

Nova Scotia Barristers' Society President R. A. Kanigsberg hands Donald Oliver the documents admitting him to the bar on May 4, 1965.

I thought of my father and how he'd spent his career as a labourer and janitor at a university. He had no university degree and indeed hadn't completed school. I didn't bring any important social or business connections. How would I possibly bring in new clients? The senior partner explained to me that if I didn't find a way to bring new business, I should not be surprised if I fell to the back of the pack for things like raises and promotions. When he was done, I thanked him and said I would work hard to try to keep up.

I sought my father's advice. He kept telling me to work hard, put in the hours, and keep my head up. I took my father's advice and determined I would bring business to the law firm, not through "family" connections but through hard work.

I spent a lot of time with my father during that period. He was getting much older. We both loved the countryside. I would often take him for long drives through some of the remote farms in our area of the Annapolis Valley. We bonded as we slowly meandered along the country roads, watching cattle grazing in the fields and pastures, seeing some of the large oat fields being caressed by the gentle wind, and simply looking at some of the well-managed farmlands. We did not have to do a lot of talking during these drives. We simply enjoyed the charms of the countryside and one another's company.

One day, when he was in his eighties, he surprised me by giving me specific directions for where he wanted to go. We came to an old farmhouse and he got out of the car and said he'd be back in a while. This was the home of a good friend he'd known for more than fifty years. He was aging and not well. My father wanted to see how he was doing and say hello—or maybe it was an implied goodbye. They spent about forty-five minutes together.

We made three such stops that day. The same thing happened at the next two stops. My father was very tired after all that, but they had all been calls he'd really wanted to make. Be assured he had been thinking about them for days before I got to drive him there. My father could sense that it was becoming increasingly difficult for him to breathe.

On April 9, 1966, my father died after a brief illness. He was eighty-two. The doctors said he died of old age and an enlarged heart. (My own current doctors from the Mayo Clinic now feel it was likely from Amyloidosis, which runs in the family.) I was in Halifax at work when he died and regretted not being with him for his last moments. I was starting my second year as a young lawyer, and his death was a jolt and a shock to me. I sensed that I, the only child of five left in Nova Scotia, had suddenly assumed a special role in assisting my mother with her needs. I had to step up to these responsibilities. I had now truly grown into manhood.

I soon found a way to bring business to the firm. I got a personal retainer in February 1968 from the president of Sir George Williams (now called Concordia) University in Montreal, Quebec. It was a golden opportunity to bring in business to the law firm. A university retainer is something sought after and cherished in the legal world. They are hard to get and I credited my father's reputation—as a university labourer!—as the reason the school had chosen me.

I learned early on that the situation I was called to deal with had multiple complications not associated with me and my specific retainer, one of which would unfortunately end in a notorious police raid on the university's computer room.

My task was to resolve the impasse between the university administration and six Black students at the centre of a heated debate about academic racism. I was to establish a forum where the six students could give evidence before a balanced, impartial tribunal or committee about their complaints regarding grades.

The case had started in spring 1968, when Rodney John, a Black student from the West Indies, filed a complaint against a white assistant biology professor named Perry Anderson. John stated Anderson discriminated against the six students by giving Black students much lower marks than their work merited. Many of the students wanted to go to medical school, so good grades were critical. The university tried to hear the complaint, but each attempt failed. The university eventually struck a hearing committee to study the accusations, but the students were not properly consulted. The committee threw out the racism complaint.

The students had some powerful evidence to support the complaint, but it was all ignored. Student Terrence Ballantyne, for example, had a lab partner in the biology class who was white. The two worked on the lab experiments together, as was standard. Ballantyne handed in his paper first and Anderson graded the work a seven out of ten. His lab partner missed the deadline and belatedly took Ballantyne's paper, copied it word for word, and submitted it as his own. He earned the highest mark in the class and didn't get a penalty for filing it late. How could a Black student and a white student get such different grades from the same teacher on the identical paper? There were many other clear examples of systemic anti-Black racism in the marking of the biology papers, and they were widely known throughout the student body.

There were thirty-three students in the Anderson biology class; thirteen were from the Caribbean. They wanted the racism addressed so they could get the grades their work merited, and so other Black students wouldn't face lower grades due to a professor's prejudice.

It wasn't long before I realized the university had two distinct and competing agendas in hiring me during the dispute. The first, easiest, reason was that they hired me to establish the framework within which the students' complaints could be brought before an objective board. The second, murkier, objective was the sit-ins. I was to represent the six students specifically, and to bring a peaceful resolution to the occupation, which lasted from January 29 to February 11.

Word went around campus that the university was failing to listen to the complaints. Students said the committee hearings had failed. Many of the students wanted to make the university hear them. Between two hundred and five hundred students of different racial backgrounds all occupied the ninth-floor computer centre on campus. The peaceful sit-in asked for a new, objective committee comprising students, faculty, and administration to listen to the students' complaints. Pressure mounted and the university struggled to deal with the growing crisis.

I flew to Montreal, checked into a motel, rolled up my sleeves, and went to work. After reading volumes of papers and other relevant documents well into the wee hours, I started my first full day in Montreal by conducting extensive interviews with the six students. I also spoke to other students with intimate knowledge of the university and with information as to what had gone on with the various other committees that had looked at this complaint. The more I learned about how systemic and widespread the racism was at Sir George, the more I realized there was so much work to do in Canada. The senior administration did not treat Black people as though they had any rights. I wanted to shed a tear and yell out. It hit me hard. Yes, the university had retained me, but interestingly I didn't report to the president, but to his legal representative. That's unusual, I thought, but I figured I'd go along with it and see how things developed. I was young, new at the job, all alone, and frankly not sure what I was really getting into. It was all a bit intimidating, but I was up for the challenge.

I walked onto the campus and headed to the computer centre. I was escorted up to the ninth floor and saw and heard a lot of things that had no relevance whatsoever to setting up a committee to hear a complaint about racial discrimination. Some of the occupiers did not seem to be students. The computer room stank of stale cigarette smoke and the old food and coffee cups piled up made it seem like a bunkhouse in the woods, not a modern computer centre on a big city campus. Newspapers cluttered the loud and noisy room.

A student speaking into a bullhorn told anyone who would listen about the recently held Black Writers Congress at nearby McGill University. The star of the congress had been Stokely Carmichael, later called Kwame Ture, the Black intellectual and principal leader of the Black Power and Black Panther movements. Suddenly I was introduced as the lawyer for the six students. Someone handed me the bullhorn. "You're Black and know about our struggle, so speak to us," the person said. Several film cameras turned their unblinking eyes toward me to record what I said and did. The newspapers scattered around the room contained rumours that police and security officials had hidden themselves in the computer centre, perhaps to stir up trouble. I felt unsettled and cautious. It was not usually part of a lawyer's job to address a heated sit-in protest of hundreds of people, unless it was to explain the law that could apply to the situation. I'm not sure how my voice sounded through the bullhorn, but I tried to keep calm and tell them I was there as legal counsel and not a civil rights activist. I told them I could not and would not become part of the sit-in or anything connected to it because part of my retainer was to satisfactorily establish a hearing tribunal so the sit-in could end. I returned the bullhorn to the first speaker. My remarks did not generate tremendous applause.

Away from the computer centre, I met often with the legal counsel for the university. He was an elderly gentleman with years of experience in law. He took this case very seriously and moved from his home to a motel suite nearer the university and dedicated himself to it full time. We met often to review paperwork and hold meetings, but he and I never had any meaningful discussions about systemic racism at Sir George, as most people called the university.

Throughout the entire process, I found the six students to be intelligent and anxious to get the occupation behind them so they could return to their everyday class routines. All six wanted to do the academic work to earn good grades. They were warm young men with charismatic personalities, and they remained dedicated to holding a peaceful occupation of the computer centre until we'd reached a mutually agreeable settlement. That included the terms of reference for a new, objective committee to hear the complaints.

I felt pressure to end the situation. I drafted a carefully worded comprehensive settlement agreement that would have seen the students withdraw peacefully from the ninth and seventh floors of the occupied building. (See Appendix A, page 211 for student's position within the agreement.) In return, the university would reform its administration and create best practices designed to rid the university of discrimination, bias, racism, or prejudice. I gave the draft to the university's lawyer and he promised to take it to the university for approval. Another two days passed.

Meanwhile, the hundreds of students occupying the two floors revolved as people joined or left. I could tell they were becoming increasingly restless and wanted a show of good faith from the university. These students were all well aware of the cavalier way in which the administration treated the Black students' complaints. The student newspaper, the *Georgian*, ran a special edition on the Anderson affair. It was clear for everyone to see that the university remained fully in support of Professor Anderson and painfully indifferent to the students' concerns.

Finally, the university's lawyer indicated to me that my agreement had been signed and we had a done deal. I advised the students to sign the agreement. At about 1 A.M., the last of them met me in my hotel room and signed it. Word spread and people started leaving the computer centre to return home, having accomplished their goals. But the university kept delaying returning the signed agreement. My hands were getting sweaty out of anxiety over the university's silence. Some students continued to occupy the computer centre. They still spoke about Black Power, student rights, and the need to fight racism. Some of the remaining protesters were Black and many were white. Many were not students at the university. There had been a lot of Marxist-Leninists, communists, and members of other radicalized groups in the computer centre for days urging on violence and obstruction to help make their ideological points. They talked about taking power back from the university administration.

The six students—my clients—took me aside and warned that if the university did not return the signed agreement within the agreed twenty-four–hour deadline, they had no control over what the occupying students and outside radicals would do in response. The atmosphere in the computer centre was volatile and becoming dangerous. I met again with university counsel and stressed the urgency of an immediate show of good faith from the university as evidence that it would keep its part of the bargain and return the signed agreement.

The deadline came and went. The university had broken its promise. Perhaps that was deliberate, given that they'd already called the riot police. Lawyers must uphold the law, and if they believe a crime is about to be committed, they must advise the participants of the legal consequences of their intended actions and withdraw from the case. Several students and outside student supporters and radicals repeatedly told me they would smash computers if the deal was not signed by the deadline. I had no choice but to advise them of their legal liability if they destroyed university property. I then tendered my resignation.

The peaceful protest ended when heavily armed and armoured riot police entered the occupied sections of the university building. I had just left the building and returned to the hotel. The police clashed with the protesters and things boiled over. People grabbed fire axes and smashed desks, chairs, and computers. Carpets were ripped up. The protestors erected barricades to stop police from getting onto the seventh and ninth floors. The elevators were shut down and the power turned off. A fire broke out in the building, flames leaping toward the ceiling, and huge black clouds of smoke billowed out of the computer centre.

Thousands of unsympathetic onlookers gathered below and gazed up at the fire. Soon, horrific chants drifted through the crowd like burning straw: "Let the niggers burn!" and "Burn, niggers, burn."

More police arrived and surrounded the few Black students in the crowd. The police were protecting them as the mob shouted threats of extreme violence. Police arrested ninety-seven people and held them in jail without bail. Of those, sixty-nine were students from Sir George, and about a third were white. Many of the rest were Black, including activist Roosevelt Douglas, the future prime minister of the Caribbean nation of Dominica. He spent several weeks in a Canadian jail after the protest.

A lot of the protesters were young and all of them were unarmed. Newspapers reported that the arrested students were separated by race—white kids in one jail, Black kids at another. Police kicked the Black people, yelled at them, and put many in the hospital. I thought of what Martin Luther King Jr. wrote in *Why We Can't Wait* in 1964:

> *Jailing the Negro was once as much a threat as the loss of a job. To any Negro who displayed a spark of manhood, a southern law-enforcement officer could say, "Nigger, watch your step, or I'll put you in jail." The Negro knew what going to jail meant. It meant not only confinement and isolation from his loved ones. It meant that at the jailhouse he could probably expect a severe beating. And it meant that his day in court, if he had it, would be a mockery of justice.*

It seemed the same was true for Black Canadians in the 1960s.

After the violence, I learned that the university had already assembled a committee to review the complaints of the six Black students. They had already concluded they could find no evidence of racism. Professor Anderson's suspension was lifted and he was fully reinstated.

The six students were good people and good students. Five of them finished their degrees and went onto post-graduate studies. Rodney John, one of the students who filed the complaint, later earned a PhD and became a clinical psychologist in Toronto. He has studied how journalists covered the riot in depth. They carefully detailed the smashed computers, yet they rarely mentioned the details of the complaint, or analyzed the systemic racism.

Many books, films, and commentaries were made about the affair, but I've never been asked, in the more than half a century that has since passed, about my role. It was interesting to me that of the dozens and dozens of news stories, reports, videos, and films made of the affair, not one journalist reached out to me, the only Black lawyer on the inside, for my inside account of what really happened. It frustrated me that, had the university honoured its word and returned the signed agreement, there would have been no violence and destruction in the computer centre. The Black students might have eventually gotten a chance to air their concerns fairly to an objective tribunal. But it ended in violence. The full story of the Black students' complaints has never been told because the racism at Sir George Williams was systemic, powerful, and widespread.

Back in Nova Scotia, I had plenty of time to analyze my own response. It was my first big case and my first out-of-province case. I was alone. Many of the protesters bombarded me with pressure to "be what I am," a Black man, and they pushed me to publicly fight for Black people when they were being wronged, no matter the consequences. I was still in my twenties, not much older than most of them. I could just imagine, of course, how difficult it would be to make cogent, persuasive legal arguments before a judge from my jail cell. But even more importantly, I had absolutely no intention of ever letting myself be put in a position where I could not uphold the rule of law. That would go against what I stood for as a lawyer and as a Canadian. Sometimes, you can't be an activist and a professional. I understood that the dividing line winds in narrow paths and is not always easy to see, let alone follow.

The whole affair was a classic case of systemic anti-Black racism. The sting and pain of systemic white privilege ran deeply through

Sir George. All the usual indicia were there: the institutional denial of reality; the cover-up or deliberate exclusion of evidence; a total lack of cooperation on ordinary basic requests; and secretly bringing in the riot police to a student demonstration that had been otherwise peaceful. The university treated the six students with contempt by showing they didn't think their views were worthy of notice, let alone cause for the university to change. From a legal point of view, getting the students to sign the agreement and then not returning the signed agreement themselves was the very epitome of a racist act.

I felt keenly aware of my grandparents' DNA in me: the DNA of Black people who had been enslaved and fought for freedom. The family of our patriarch, Moses Oliver, who was the visionary. My family made it clear to me on our Wolfville farm that whatever other social and political activities I pursued, I must always remember to devote my life to fighting—and ultimately defeating—racism and white privilege. I submitted my legal bill to the university. They paid it promptly.

Chapter Six

THE BLACK CULTURAL CENTRE

THE LATE 1960S AND EARLY 1970S WERE TUMULTUOUS YEARS for Nova Scotia Blacks. It was a period of transformation and awakening after more than four hundred years of slavery and oppression. The American civil rights movement, led by Rev. Martin Luther King Jr., was the pinnacle of non-violent social/political uprisings around the world, all of which had a direct influence on movements in Nova Scotia. The Sir George Williams "computer party," where Black students rose up to assert their rights, had its influence and impact in Nova Scotia as well.

Nova Scotia Blacks were very divided, made up of an estimated thirty-four thousand people living in more than thirty little communities around the province. Apart from the church, there was very little to unite community with community or to facilitate a meaningful form of communication with a common voice. You will recall that in the time of slavery, mothers and fathers were often separated, their children taken from them and put on another plantation, as a means to divide and conquer. Black refugees brought the impact of that history with them to the province, and the outright discrimination continued by the white British. In short, the theory was "keep them divided and apart," and "don't let them organize." Black people, for instance, were rarely given their promised land grants, or what they might receive would be a ten-acre licence to farm on extremely rocky, almost unusable, terrain. So they were forced to move on.

Life for Blacks in Nova Scotia at that time was appalling. Disproportionate numbers of Black youth were in jail for crimes they did not commit, or for very minor crimes, certainly much higher numbers than white youth who'd committed the same crimes. It was difficult for Black women, men, and youth to find any type of suitable full-time employment. There were insufficient numbers of Black doctors to service the unique medical needs of the community. Segregation between Black and white was rampant. This was a time when little Black children could not be buried in a "white" cemetery.

In 1968, I worked with Gus Wedderburn, who was then head of the Nova Scotia Association for the Advancement of Coloured People. I was the vice-president. We became aware of a tragedy in which a three-year-old girl had died, and her local cemetery in St. Croix, Hants County, would not bury her because she was Black. The white residents of St. Croix had passed a bylaw in 1907 that barred the burial of Black people in that cemetery—even children. It was utterly astounding. We went public with our concerns. St. Croix rescinded that law a few weeks after our outcry and the child was laid to rest. The St. Croix law was shocking to many people, but for much of Nova Scotia's history, it was not permissible to bury

Don's sister Eugenie became the head of dietetics at a hospital in Hamilton, Bermuda; she eventually rose to the top of the administrative ranks at the hospital.

Black people alongside the "general population," which meant white people. Instead, Black people had to bury family and friends in the spaces along the outer edges of graveyards.

It was part of the province's widespread segregation. Some of it was formally enshrined in laws and some of it was in the hearts and minds of individual people. Many white barbers, for example, would not cut a Black man's hair. I personally experienced that in North End Halifax when I approached a shop with four empty chairs and one of the grey-haired barbers came to the door and waved me on. "We don't cut your kind of hair," he told me.

Churches and schools were still segregated, long after segregation was declared illegal in 1954. Orphanages were segregated by race. Our military was rigorously segregated. Athletic and sports facilities used by the public were closed to Blacks on strictly racial grounds. In public schools, Black students were most often

Genie as a young woman in Bermuda.

stereotyped by white teachers as predatory, objectionable, and without educational value. Young Black women could still not get into the Victoria General Hospital's nursing school to complete the requirement for a registered nurse designation merely because of the colour of their skin. Halifax wouldn't send snowplows or road graders to Africville, but it was still collecting the residents' taxes, and later it would be sending bulldozers to destroy the community.

Life was hard. There was little room in many Black lives for hope. It was hard to dream a happy dream. Many of our people had hit bottom and were trying to bounce back. One wondered, what would it take for things to get better? We lived in anticipation. Various levels of government, many social and charitable organizations, many clergymen, and countless others took steps to stop the bleeding in the Black communities and to try to find solutions.

My sisters Shirley and Genie both married men from Bermuda, which led me to visit the country in the late 1950s and early 1960s. I expected culture shock, but instead fell head-over-heels in love with the tiny, enchanting island. The former English colony is decorated with beautiful pastel homes along the shoreline. It feels wonderful to splash in the warm, foamy waves on a pink sandy beach. It is a bit of paradise for me.

The last thing I expected to find there was Black Power. That was the true culture shock. In Bermuda, I found that Black people were united, they knew their culture and heritage, and they led and ran their own organizations to build community.

As I walked along the sunny streets of Hamilton, the capital, I was shocked and pleasantly surprised when I saw, for the first time in my life, Black economic power, Black financial power, and Black cultural power. I had never experienced this in Canada. In Wolfville, we were the only Black people. Here, it seemed like everyone was Black. Black people started businesses. Black people owned the stores and shopped in the stores. Black people chauffeured rich people around, and some of the rich people were Black too. Most of the government was Black. The head of the bank was Black. Many surgeons were Black. Black people were the majority in Bermuda and you could see the impact everywhere. It was so different than home in Nova Scotia, when at the time we still had segregated schools, churches, and businesses. Bermuda showed me that Black people can do anything. I was stunned and in awe of this exercise of Black Power. It filled me with a secret glee and delight.

And yet Bermuda was still poisoned by racism everywhere you turned. White people were a minority, but they still controlled a majority of the wealth and power. Some families had built their wealth as slave owners. Some white people still thought of Black people as slaves. With white privilege, they defined Black people as lazy, apathetic, dumb, and shiftless "good timers," despite abundant evidence to the contrary. I returned to Nova Scotia eager to apply the Bermuda lessons of viable economic power to our scattered Black communities. We, too, could do anything. It brought me hope.

During this period of general upheaval and hopelessness, one person seemed to have his finger on the Black pulse more than anyone else. He was my stepbrother, Rev. Dr. W. P. Oliver. My father's son from his first marriage, and he had been largely brought up by a single parent—my father, after he and his wife divorced. William, or Bill, as I usually called him, was born in Wolfville in the same house where I was born and raised, but was twenty-six years older than me. I always looked up to him, amazed by his athleticism—he was an all-star in hockey and football, and captained both teams. He loved to run. He loved to learn, too, and graduated with two degrees: a bachelor of arts and a bachelor of divinity, both from Acadia University. The family's innate drive for education was an essential part of his DNA.

In 1936, two years before my birth, William married Pearleen Borden. Over their fifty-three–year marriage, they raised five children. It was a union forged in heaven. Pearleen worked alongside Bill, and often raced in front of him, opening those doors that prevented Black women from becoming registered nurses, for example. In 1945, she waged a personal campaign to have a book called *Little Black Sambo*, which contained racist and insulting images of Black people, removed from the education curriculum in our province's schools.

William was pastor of several churches in the province before he took over pastoring at what was then called Cornwallis Street Baptist Church—now called New Horizons—in Halifax. It was the very church where my grandfather, Rev. Dr. William White, had ministered for twenty-five years. It is considered the mother church of the African United Baptist Association. Pearleen was the first woman moderator of the African United Baptist Church. She and William both worked to develop several youth programs and gained support from the broader community. In 1962, William was elected president of the Maritime Baptist Convention, the first

African Nova Scotian to hold such a position. He had also been pastor of Beechville Baptist Church since 1937, a position he held until his death in 1989. Throughout all this ministering and church work, he was employed with the Adult Education Division for the province, and he worked as regional representative of education in Black communities in Nova Scotia. This proved to be a very useful experience, because in each of the communities he worked in he met the elders, the leaders, and the youth, and learned first-hand about their most pressing needs. He could take this back to the province in order to develop public policies.

Like the other children of Clifford Oliver, William knew instinctively the importance of education, particularly as an agent of social change. One of his fond remembrances of the regional education job was the Lighted Schoolhouse program. That program kept schools open at night and hired teachers to teach adult literacy skills. Giving people a better education helped to build a sense of hope.

As an adult, I had a wonderful opportunity to work with my stepbrother on a few different projects and, in each case, I learned a lot. He believed there was dignity in work. He understood the need of Black parents who wanted to own their own home. We worked together in Beechville, a suburb of Halifax, where William had ministered for decades. I did a lot of pro bono legal work for Black people throughout Nova Scotia. One time it was for a small, Black-run co-op housing project. I tried to strengthen the land titles so everyone could own their own homes. My stepbrother gave overall direction to the project, including negotiating for some of the building materials such as bricks. Several families working cooperatively built nice houses, planted lawns, and had their own flower gardens, which brought great joy and pride and a sense of fulfillment and happiness. Just imagine— their children would have their own warm room in their own home to study in and do their schoolwork in during the cold winter months. I believe one of the roads near that project is named Oliver Way.

When there were Black youth he was working with who had legal problems, I was frequently called in to provide help and advice. Sometimes it was a lot more than advice: once, it was a for a jury trial on a murder charge. A young person had been charged with the attempted murder of his brother by firing a loaded gun at him in anger. The trial went before a jury and I represented the accused throughout. The four-day trial ended with a not-guilty verdict.

William and I both loved to fish, and we enjoyed heading to the province's rivers, streams, and lakes to catch trout. I lived then on the Pleasant River, renowned for canoeing and as one of the better trout-fishing rivers around. One beautiful spring day my big brother William visited my farm and we decided to go fishing. I toured him quickly around the gardens and trees as the morning sun lifted over the river and a pleasant breeze drifted in from the west. We got dressed in our fishing gear, checked out our rods and reels one last time, made sure we had some provisions for the day, and before we knew it, it was time to leave. I had arranged for one of my local friends to take us in his boat to some of the good fishing pools for the day. I could see the glee in Bill's eyes the moment we started downriver in the boat. We saw and heard a beaver splash into the river at one stage, and later saw a lot of ducks taking off and landing. We fished all the good holes as we meandered downriver, stopping often to try to place our bait or flies right where the fish should be feeding. The big fish were not doing a lot of biting that day. The water was a little high and still quite cool, though the morning sun was changing that.

A few kilometres downriver we anchored the boat near shore. Bill, my friend, and I set up at three different pools on the river and cast for trout. We had a grand time exploring the countryside in the fresh air—so much so we barely noticed the blackflies that were determined to eat us alive. As we were fishing I heard William upriver calling out, "Got one!" and a few minutes later, "Another one!" The trout were hungry and we had a fifteen-minute feeding frenzy as the river boiled with fish who jumped for our flies. And just as quickly as it started, it stopped. The waters calmed and our rods stilled. We got back into the boat and tried different parts of the river. Nothing. The moment had come and gone. My stepbrother and I loved the open hours of conversation and bonded more like a father and son than brothers. I felt so proud to be his kin.

When we got back home to the farm, I lightly breaded and pan-fried some of our bounty. We added some vegetables from my garden. I could see that my big brother had difficulty expressing that he'd had such a great time. He wrote in my guest book: "You're a chip off the old block," particularly in relation to my vegetable and flower gardens that reminded him so much of our father.

Bill's biggest dream, he'd told me, was to create a cultural centre for Black Nova Scotians. He'd been instrumental in founding the NSAACP and the Black United Front, organizations that helped many in the Black community overcome problems. But there was still something missing: hope. We needed an education centre for learning and training that, at the same time, would openly display the evidence of four hundred years of toil on the part of Black Nova Scotians. We needed the art and the artifacts to show and illustrate the road from bondage.

In his years ministering to young Black people, William had seen that theme repeated. Many had no hope, no role models, and no sense of history. They would look up, but they had no Black heroes to look up to. And yet the Black heroes of history were our ancestors. Young people did not understand the history of slavery or the sacrifices and tribulations of our forefathers and mothers. They did not know where they came from. The thinking was that if our youth knew and understood their history and could look up to their Black heroes, then they could see a better way forward. Our ancestors would give us light and hope for the future. The great Black hero Marcus Garvey, who once delivered an important speech in Nova Scotia, wrote that "a people without knowledge of its history is like a tree without roots." Garvey's son, carrying on his teachings, recently said that we needed a transformation of consciousness about who we were, where we came from and what we can be. My stepbrother wanted to build a museum for our roots.

In a biography of Dr. Oliver called *Born with a Call*, my step-brother recalled that when he was a schoolboy of eleven, he had a conversation with an older friend, and that conversation stayed with him for years. His friend said, "Billy, what are you going to be?"

He shyly responded, "I don't know."

Without missing a beat, his friend said, "You can be anything that you want to be." As a grown man, wise in years, that was the message he wanted to deliver to Black Nova Scotian youth through a cultural centre: You can be anything you want to be. It would be a place where they could look, see, and read about how other Blacks, in very trying circumstances, were able to rise up and say, "I now feel I can be anything I want to be."

Dr. Oliver had a profound influence on me. And as life has it, that influence seems to grow more with each passing year. He had a quiet softness in his approach to dealing with people; he was always prepared to give them another chance, to wait them out. He gave everyone time to express themselves. I tried to make that an intrinsic part of all that I did in my life. But he was unique and it was hard to follow his kindness. It was written, upon his death, that "always he bore the mark of gentleness and dignity. He was a reformer who quietly and unobtrusively got things done."

We spoke constantly of education. Our family had lived on the grounds of Acadia University for nearly a century and we all knew the power of an education. He and I wondered what permanent things we could do now that would help more Black youth get a good education. How could we inspire them? How could we pave a path for them?

In 1972, he shared with me a draft proposal to create a cultural education centre. I was fascinated by the concept. This would be an important first for Canada. It might be the vehicle to provide some permanent hope to our youth. If they were learning about Black people, perhaps that would motivate them to learn more about their culture and history. The past could help build the future. Knowing the sacrifices their Black ancestors had made for them, perhaps they would find a new pride in their identity. But I couldn't imagine how we could fund it, build it, and even persuade the Black communities of Nova Scotia to adopt it. And then how would we keep funding it year after year?

We found land—a space north of Dartmouth and near the Black-majority community of Cherry Brook, across the road from an orphanage known as the Home for Colored Children. We hired architects to draw the blueprints. We got estimates for the construction cost. I set out to raise money, and gathered hundreds of thousands of dollars from major corporations. The provincial government added money and many other resources. With the initial financing in place, crews started building the two-storey, 18,000–square foot centre. In 1977, the province passed a law called the Society for the Protection and Preservation of Black Culture in Nova Scotia. I worked closely with legislative draftsmen in the province and, indeed, held the pen in the drafting of the "purpose" and other clauses of the bill. A friend named Sharon Ross played a crucial role in getting the dozens of Black communities enthusiastic and onside with the project. She was the principal administrator and manager of the entire project for years.

It took eleven years of hard work. Finally, in 1983, the Black Cultural Centre was opened to the public. It was a jubilant day. This was the fulfillment of Dr. Oliver's biggest dream. It was a day of happiness, joy, and triumph for Black communities throughout Nova Scotia. In this cultural centre, our Black youth could find

Donald Oliver with his nephews Jules and Leslie Oliver at the Black Cultural Centre in Cherry Brook, Nova Scotia. On this day, Don was being recognized with a place on the centre's Wall of Honour.

stories of Black heroes and Black role models who made a difference in Canada. How could the myth of Black inferiority survive such an education? I was honoured to be elected the founding president of the society that would operate the centre.

Our Black Cultural Centre was the first of its kind in Canada. It housed a museum, archives, library, art gallery, an education complex, and an amphitheatre. It chronicled the four hundred–year history of Black people in Nova Scotia, bearing witness to their stories of toil, effort, perseverance, and above all, hope. And they had achieved this in the face of almost immeasurable adversity. We had created a cultural legacy that would otherwise have remained unknown and inaccessible to Canadians and the rest of the world. My stepbrother was a true visionary. Moses Oliver would have been proud.

Chapter Seven

LINC

MY EARLY YEARS AS A LAWYER WERE HARD WORK AT THE magistrates' court, trying to build a reputation as the lawyer to hire, and to catch the eye of the senior lawyers. I also started to get some other small cases in my office on adoption, a minor land dispute, a small motor vehicle accident with injuries, divorce and custody matters, and employment discrimination issues. I was soon taking trials and the occasional appeal, but most of all getting to feel at ease in the courts. I studied how other lawyers conducted themselves before the court and with other counsel and, even more importantly, how judges decided cases. I built up a personal inner library from my observations and conclusions on these matters that I could call on for years to come. The family law cases started to roll in: separations, custody disputes, divorces, divisions of matrimonial property—all sorts of different cases—and I soon found myself buried under an avalanche of work. I didn't want to spend my career in family law, yet it started to feel unavoidable.

But that problem resolved itself. One of the insurance companies I had already done dozens of trials for around the province was interested in having me take on a large and complicated civil case in the neighbouring province of Prince Edward Island. This was a most unusual request. The common rule was to practice only where you are registered. I was licensed to practice only in Nova Scotia, but the insurer insisted that they wanted me to be the lawyer in charge of the carriage of the case. We made a formal application and asked PEI's regulatory board for special leave to allow me to take a case in their jurisdiction. They agreed. I went to court there and won the case. The insurer was pleased and I started to be sent even more good files.

That insurance company had claims and lawsuits all around the province. I did a number of trials over several years at the Supreme Court in Cape Breton. There were several courthouses around the province and I am certain that during my time practising law I had an opportunity to try cases in most of them. Some were small, local, rural courthouses in places like Bridgewater, Liverpool, Yarmouth, Digby, Kentville, Annapolis, Amherst, Antigonish, and throughout Cape Breton. Those courthouses might hear cases at the level of magistrates' court, county court, or Supreme Court. A number of mine were Supreme Court matters.

I found it enchanting to be in some of those rural venues. In Annapolis, for instance, they have a small country courthouse near the edge of town. I liked trying cases there; it's tranquil and peaceful, and it is relatively close to the famous Annapolis Royal Historic Gardens. On breaks or early evenings, I would wander through the beautiful, seventeen-acre historic gardens, which were grand in design and overlooked a tidal river valley. The gardens have the largest collection of roses in eastern Canada. What a wonderful place to spend time away from the courthouse.

I was truly blessed in my practice. Agents and brokers heard of my work in court and referred a few new files to me for different companies, opening new doors for me. I had a habit of winning cases.

In motor vehicle and other insurance cases, I usually represented the defence, but at times I would take plaintiffs' files, too. I loved going to court. I loved the pretrial preparation that included sending out subpoenas, preparing and submitting a pretrial brief to the court, and preparing witnesses and various demonstrative pieces of evidence that would be admitted as exhibits. On a major trial I made sure I knew precisely what recent cases my judge had tried before this one, and how she or he tended to rule. I tried to make sure I knew as much as I could about counsel on the other side as well.

One day, I learned what one other lawyer really thought of me. I was ready to go to court, but the other lawyer was late delivering certain critical documents to me that had been ordered by the court. I phoned that lawyer's office to ask when I could expect to receive them. The documents arrived within an hour. There was a note accidentally still pinned to them: "Here, take this over to the spook." That would be me—evidently, the sight of a Black man working as a lawyer was so rare, they felt confident that was all they needed to say. I learned a lot about that particular lawyer that day. That was certainly not the only such experience I encountered at the bar.

Throughout the 1970s, I tried dozens of Supreme Court cases, some of which led to new laws, and thus many of my cases ended up reported in the important and widely read *Dominion Law Reports*.

But in the early 1980s I got another chilling reminder that, no matter who I was as a person, no matter what I accomplished as a professional, to some people I'd never be anything but a Black man. I am aware of one client who was referred to me for advice, which I gave, but who later complained to the senior partner that he refused to take advice from a Black man. The senior partner told him that if he did not accept my counsel, he would not be referred to any other lawyer in the firm. He left.

Around that time, my sister Shirley and her husband, Clarence James, were visiting me in Halifax. Shirley and my other older sister, Genie, had taken science degrees at Acadia, and both had to do internships so they could practice as dieticians. There was jubilation and celebration in our Wolfville home when Shirley was accepted as a student intern at the Massachusetts General Hospital in Boston for a year, beginning in September 1956. She was the first of the five of us to leave home, which naturally brought a few tears. In 1957, she'd gone to the big city of Montreal to take a job as a dietician at the Montreal General Hospital. One day she'd had a chance meeting with a brilliant young Black student from Bermuda who was studying for his MD and planned to stay on in Montreal to complete his residency in general surgery. It was Clarence James, who had entered McGill on a big scholarship. They started a romance that culminated in their return to Wolfville in 1958 to be married at the Baptist church. In 1963, they moved to Bermuda with their two young children, Johnny and Joanne. Clarence was a surgeon and politician in Bermuda. He was a brilliant general surgeon and would become the country's first Black finance minister and deputy premier, and was celebrated as one of modern Bermuda's most important nation-builders.

We were dressed for the big occasion of our dinner in honour of Shirley and Clarence in Halifax. They had been visiting Wolfville at the time and had driven to Halifax to meet me. In the car were my mother, my sister, my brother-in-law, and a friend of my mother's. We parked at Hogie's Steakhouse and BBQ on Quinpool Road. We went inside at about 5:30 P.M. and saw that some tables were already occupied. It was a popular spot. We chose a table for six near the front window. Three empty tables for four surrounded us on three sides. I tried to catch the waitress's eye to ask for menus, but had no success. The good mood started to fade.

The three empty tables next to us filled up over the next fifteen minutes. They all got menus and glasses of water. I stood up to better catch the attention of the waitress so we could get our menus. She avoided my entreaties. Nearly thirty minutes passed. Everyone else was eating. Our table was without even a glass of fresh water. Suddenly, a tall man—presumably either the manager or owner—stormed over to our table, his face red, stained by an angry frown. He jabbed his finger at me, my mother, her friend, my sister, and her esteemed husband.

"You people can sit there as long as you want," he called out loud enough for the entire restaurant to hear. "We don't serve Negroes in this restaurant."

We were in shock. No one said anything. No other patrons objected. As a lawyer, I felt an argument for why we should be served rising in my throat, but I looked at my mother and realized I couldn't put her through more emotional strain. Even if I won my case and got them to serve us, what might they put in our food? I had an urge to bang the chairs and make a noisy exit to challenge the insult, but instead calmly helped my mother and the others to leave.

This overt racism against Black people in all aspects of our daily lives happened to Black people in Nova Scotia frequently. I felt so powerless. As an officer of the court, I could not stand up in the restaurant and encourage other patrons to protest with me in an act that could in some way be construed as infringing on the criminal law. I later wrote a strong letter of protest. It changed nothing. White privilege prevailed.

❖

In the late 1970s I met the person who would become one of my most important Black mentors: Lincoln Alexander. He is certainly one of Canada's best-known and most respected Black men.

He would eventually have skyways, schools, community centres, and scholarships named after him, and a national day of celebration. His parents had come to Canada from the Caribbean. His mother, Mae, was from Jamaica and was a major influence on his life. She worked as a maid. His father, Lincoln, after whom he was named, was a porter on the Canadian Pacific Railway; he was from Saint Vincent and the Grenadines.

Lincoln grew up and attended school in Toronto. He served with the Royal Canadian Air Force during the Second World War, from 1942 to 1945, and entered McMaster University when he returned to Canada. He graduated from Osgoode Hall Law School in 1953. There were not many Blacks in Canada graduating in law at that time. He had more difficulty than I did in finding a place to do his articles and on being admitted to the bar to practice. Getting over each of those hurdles was in itself a feat.

I first met Lincoln through politics. I was the national director of legal affairs for the Conservative Party at the time and served as such in the general elections of 1972, '74, '79, '80, '84, and '88. I had been working with the chief electoral officer since 1972 on important new election expense legislation that governed campaign spending limits for individuals and for the party itself. It passed Parliament in 1974, and the party executive, under the leadership of the national director and my good friend, Paul Curley, was determined that every candidate running for the party clearly understand the new spending limits and run their campaigns in strict compliance. Part of my job, initiated by Mr. Stanfield with a nod from his chief of staff and my friend, Graham Scott, was to travel across Canada and instruct all our party's provincial legal counsel and candidates' counsel on the details of the law as well as the official party position on how these new expense laws were to be interpreted and applied.

I was in the riding of Hamilton West during the 1979 campaign, giving lectures and answering questions on the new legislation, when I met Lincoln. He was a tall man with a big personal presence. He was a great conversationalist and had a telling word or expression for every circumstance. He always looked distinguished, with his moustache and winning smile. He had a calming personality so everyone around him always felt relaxed and very much at ease. We had many opportunities to talk and get to know one another through politics.

He had run for a seat in the House of Commons and been elected in 1968 as the MP from Hamilton West. Not only was he the first Black man elected to the Parliament of Canada, but in 1979, when he ran for office again, he became the first Black federal minister of labour, appointed by the Right Honourable Joe Clarke.

After politics, he was appointed the first Black chair of the workers compensation board from 1980 to 1985. He was next appointed lieutenant-governor of Ontario from 1985 to 1991. He was the first Black person in Canadian history to serve in that vice-regal position and he served with great distinction. He also served five terms as chancellor of the University of Guelph (1991 to 2007).

It seemed that Linc was loved by almost everyone he met, and by the thousands more who watched in awe and read about him from afar. He received many, many honours and awards, certainly far too many to mention in this little memoir. He was a lawyer, a politician, a cabinet minister, a bureaucrat, and the Queen's official representative in Canada's largest province. All the people he met had warmth in their heart for him and thousands wanted their pictures taken with him. Rarely was a bad word said about him.

I saved many of the private notes he sent me over three decades, and they all contained words of encouragement. I was so proud of him and what he meant to Canada, and equally proud that he wanted to be a mentor to me from afar.

He was a tall, elegantly groomed Black man, and yet the majority of Ontarians he served didn't seem to see his colour—or did not see it as a barrier. They never seemed to need to dig into their pockets and pull out their white-privilege badge and flash it with pride. No. None of that at all. I have spent hours thinking about his natural charm, and his ability to get along with anyone—his personal way of chilling and killing white privilege. It was reminiscent of my early days with my family in Wolfville in the 1950s and 1960s, when we were able to get along so well and be tolerated as equals in our all-white community.

In a note to me about racism he said, "The problem lies in loss of job opportunities, economic deprivation, and myths and attitudes that exist by whites regarding people of colour. That's the problem." So all was not peaches and cream; Lincoln's own personal experiences had taught him that racism runs even deeper than that. Like me, he had racial ups and down in school, university, at work, and at play. For instance, during Lincoln's third year in law school at Osgoode Hall, Dean Ernest Smalley-Baker, in a class of 250 students, suddenly said, "It was like looking for a nigger in a woodpile." Linc waited for the dean to take questions. Linc raised himself to his full height and asked, "What's the meaning of the expression 'nigger in a woodpile?'" The atmosphere in the classroom grew tense immediately. While still on his feet, Lincoln reminded them that the dean was in a position of authority and that a leader has to lead, and suggested that he should not use such disrespectful comments without even thinking about them.

Linc expected to be failed because of those particular comments, but he passed and graduated. Later, when he saw the dean at a social event, Linc told him that he was surprised he had passed. The dean, in turn, said he felt personally offended by Lincoln's surprise. Was Linc challenging his intellectual integrity? Linc was one of the top students, so of course he would pass. I shall never forget how Linc summed up the affair in his memoir, *Go to School, You're a Little Black Boy*:

Senator Donald Oliver in his Ottawa office, 1992.

Senator Donald Oliver and his wife, Linda, with Prime Minister Stephen Harper during a reception at the prime minister's residence at 24 Sussex Drive in Ottawa.

Senator Donald Oliver with Prime Minister Brian Mulroney at an Ottawa reception circa 2004.

Don and his new bride, Linda MacLellan, on their wedding day at the farm, August 29, 1981.

Don and Linda's daughter, Carolynn, on the day of their wedding.

A family photo from Don and Linda's wedding day. Left to right: Linda Oliver; Don Oliver; Don's mother, Helena Oliver; Don's sister-in-law, Pearleen Oliver, and her husband and Don's brother, Rev. Dr. W. P. Oliver.

In a lead-up meeting in Washington to the G20 summit in the fall of 2009, Prime Minister Stephen Harper invited Senator Donald Oliver to meet US President Barack Obama. The three are shown here after the Senator's private meeting with President Obama in the Oval Office.

Senator Donald Oliver speaks with Governor General Adrienne Clarkson during a reception at the Centre Block, the main parliamentary building in Ottawa, in 2000.

Donald Oliver at a reception in Ottawa with the Right Honourable Robert Stanfield in 1972. Stanfield became a mentor to Oliver and their relationship lasted several decades.

Retired south shore Senator, Honorable Donald Oliver QC , receives the Canada Sesquicentennial Medal from Nova Scotia Senator Wanda Thomas Bernard and Speaker George Furey.

Queens County senator honoured in Ottawa

Retired south shore Senator, Honorable Donald Oliver QC , was among nine Nova Scotians awarded the Canada Sesquicentennial Medal by Nova Scotia Senator Wanda Thomas Bernard and Speaker George Furey at a ceremony held in the Senate chambers in Ottawa recently.

The citation says the medal is conferred " in recognition of your valuable service to the nation."

The Senate Speaker told those assembled that the purpose was to honor Canadians whose generosity, dedication, volunteerism and selfless service have meant so much to so many.

The anniversary program said the following about the retired senator: Donald H. Oliver, The first African Nova Scotian appointed to the senate of Canada, where he served for 23 years. Senator Oliver's most notable work may be his commitment to addressing issues of diversity, racism and discrimination. He is a role model for African Nova Scotians and he is committed to social justice issues and advocacy for Nova Scotia human rights.

Retired Senator Oliver had a distinguished career in parliament where he chaired several standing committees in the senate and rose to be Speaker Pro Tempore of the Senate of Canada.

In addition to devoting his career to fostering policies to promote fairness, diversity, and equality for all, he served on more than 25 charitable boards and organizations throughout the province and was awarded five Honorary Degrees from Canadian universities, acknowledging his pioneering work to combat racism and injustice.

The retired senator remains active from his farm home serving several health and community causes in Lunenburg and Queens Counties.

This clipping marks the day Senator Donald Oliver received the Canada 150 Medal for unselfish service to Community and Country; it was presented to him by Senate Speaker George Furey accompanied by Senator Wanda Thomas Bernard.

Senator Donald Oliver was awarded a number of honorary degrees over the years, including this Doctor of Laws (honoris causa) from Dalhousie University in Halifax in 2003.

(ABOVE) *Then and now: the humble century-old farmhouse Senator Donald Oliver bought in rural Nova Scotia; it was gradually renovated into his dream home, complete with idyllic gardens, a state-of-the-art kitchen, a wine cellar, a home theatre, and other amenities.*

(BELOW) *Senator Donald Oliver has a deep love of food and wine, and he loves to cook—so much so that he took an intensive course at Le Cordon Bleu Culinary School in London, England. Here, he looks very comfortable in his home kitchen.*

It was a good lesson in the difference between being Black in a white world and being a member of that majority. As a Black, I was so suspicious of the fragility of my rights that it seemed perfectly logical I could be failed for my impertinence. To him, his academic integrity and independence were unassailable, yet he could make a comment in class like that without grasping its impact.

The racism was so ingrained that people didn't even realize how wrong and hurtful it could be, and how countless thousands of Blacks in Canada have to endure such pain in silence for fear of reprisals. Linc certainly helped me find my way in work and in life as a Black person.

When it came to finding my way as a lawyer, I was lucky and privileged to try cases with David Chipman and Ron Pugsley, the senior litigation counsel in our firm. Both became Supreme Court judges, and I think neither, while practicing, had any rival in any courtroom east of Montreal. I had the thrill of working side by side with them for years, which was the highlight of my legal career at the firm.

I did a number of trials with David. Between us it was mostly work, but a deep and lasting personal friendship gradually arose. We were both Progressive Conservatives, and in our firm that was rare, most of the others being Liberal. David had been a brilliant student in university, graduating as the gold medalist, and he had almost a photographic memory for details and facts. He loved music, theatre, and bridge. He was intense and competitive but clearly understood the complexities and uncertainties of any trial. Anything could happen, and our job was to manage the unknown.

One time, David and I were defending in court during a three-week-long trial about a storm sewer line that had been installed for a municipality, but which didn't meet the pressure test. What was to blame? David hired an engineer who showed it was not negligence or faulty installation for the sewer line, but rather a problem with the huge cement pipes. The engineer built his own template and measured the pipe, and found the same problem that had plagued the real sewer. The pipes were out of round. The male end and the female end of the pipe had been improperly manufactured. It sounds simple, but to get the handmade template into court, we had to win many complicated points of evidence. There were also issues about expert witnesses. Jim Kent, the engineer we hired, had an assistant, a Black lawyer and engineer named Tony Ross, whom I got to know quite well. It was wonderful seeing another Black lawyer in the courts.

The trial helped me mature as a courtroom lawyer. It sharpened my mind to the essential parts of the trial. It taught me lessons about how to be prepared for the unknown. It taught me to ask only the questions that were needed to be asked, and to ask them in a clear, precise way. In later years, when I was a member of the Senate of Canada sitting on a number of powerful committees, this training helped me frame my questions precisely for a wide variety of witnesses who appeared before us.

Being a Black man in the largest law firm in Atlantic Canada had its ups and downs, and I kept moving forward, eventually rising to the rank of senior partner in the 1980s. There were not many Black lawyers anywhere in Canada who could claim the same career path to the top. It was exceedingly difficult for all of us. In later life, several Supreme Court judges whom I had appeared before continued to exchange calls and correspondence with me on subjects such as diversity and other public policy issues I was working on. This was done out of mutual friendship and respect. You could not sit on the Supreme Court bench for long without realizing how deep and systemic anti-Black racism was in Nova Scotia. Many of their letters to me expressed that understanding.

I had made several good friends in the firm throughout the years and even now, as my days are coming to an end, I can think of a dozen lawyers who became highly cherished friends. David Miller began as a tenant and became a great personal friend as he rose to be one of the most brilliant civil litigation lawyers in the firm, and indeed, the entire province; my long-time personal counsellor and respected friend Donald Murray; and my annual golfing-firm foursome, Doug Mathews, Jim Cowan, and John McFarlane. Others, like Charles Reagh, have been a constant source of help and assistance. It was a great firm in spite of itself.

David Chipman received his call from Ottawa in 1987 and he would retire from the law firm and accept his richly merited appointment to the Supreme Court bench, a great honour for him. As was the tradition, the firm planned to hold a black-tie dinner in his honour to thank him for his years of faithful service. Well, as it would happen, on the day of the gala dinner I had a major jury trial for one of my good clients, Petro-Canada. After a couple of days of evidence, the jury was charged by the presiding judge in the afternoon and went out to begin deliberations around 4:30 P.M. There was no way I would make David's dinner. I phoned the senior partners and explained that the jury had just gone out to begin their deliberations; they could come back to the court any time to ask a question or to have a portion of the evidence played back to them. I had to be there. The jury could be out for twenty minutes or for four or five hours. No one knew.

Well, after a lengthy consultation and deliberation, the jury returned with a verdict in favour of my client. I had won. Everyone was happy. I would be able to get to the celebratory dinner, even if it was almost over. I can't tell you how pleased I was to whisper to David with a smile, "We won." David understood perfectly what I had been going through and was happy for me. He and his wife, Carolyn, remain great friends.

But as I approached my middle years, I was becoming keenly aware of a profound absence in my life: I had no family of my own.

Chapter Eight

MARRIAGE AND THE SENATE

AS THE 1980S STARTED AND I WAS IN MY EARLY FORTIES, I FELT as though I had been running around the world for decades, trying to discover just where I could fit in best and what I should be doing to help make Canada an even better place to live. For some time, I had been coming to the realization that some things—a lot of important things—simply could not be done by one person alone. It would really be nice to have a partner. I often thought it was odd to find a bachelor in charge of a major corporation or a huge start-up initiative even though I, too, was a bachelor.

Not only that, but it was my view that democracy was strongest when it was tied together by loving families in which children could grow up with open and free family discussions and, in their own ways, contribute to the political process. The family is the nucleus of civilization and the basic social unit of society. I had held those views for years. But with teaching at three different universities, carrying a busy civil litigation law practice, chairing and sitting on dozens of not-for-profit boards, working with the Black community on a wide variety of different causes, trying to set up a farming operation an hour and a half from home, giving lectures and participating in panels on tolerance and diversity, and being directly involved in a number of business enterprises such as selling trucks, construction, and mining equipment and building a real estate company with many dozens of residential units, I was overextended. I could not manage it all alone.

I was not looking for a business partner; I already had managers for the real estate things. Rather, I thought it would be nice to have a partner to share some of the beautiful things in the world with. To have a family and enjoy watching our children grow into adults. To have someone to stroll art galleries with, and someone to sit quietly with in front of a fireplace reading a book and listening to classical music. To have someone in whom I felt a sense of ultimate trust and kinship. And, in my case, to have someone who loved food and entertaining. I'd had girlfriends since my university days and had dated throughout the 1960s and 1970s, but none of those relationships had been long-lasting.

One day I met someone who touched me in a different way. Her name was Linda MacLellan. I felt it in my heart, but needed to be sure. I wasn't about to rush into it. We started with casual dates, then a lot more dates. Linda and I both worked in downtown Halifax and I invited her to lunch at my house. I had planned in advance what I was going to serve and had prepared some things the night before, knowing we would only have about forty minutes before returning to work. I served a Jean-Georges–type shrimp salad with two sauces, a hot and a cold. We sat down and began to eat.

"If I were serving this salad, I would have left out the lemon and truffle sauce, and it would have heightened the enjoyment of the lovely shrimp," she said.

Well! What an interesting observation. We talked about it more in the car going back to work. She was not reluctant to express an opinion on things, particularly food, which certainly was my biggest hobby. We grew closer and everything between us made perfect sense but many people must have doubted it could ever work. She was white and I was Black. She was divorced and had a young child; I was a forty-three-year-old bachelor. She was Roman Catholic; I was Baptist. She was a free spirit and was not a planner or record-keeper of any sort; I had an organized structure to my life and lived by my daily to-do list. On the surface, it seemed like a poor match. In reality, it was perfect for us.

I already had a lovely five-bedroom home for us in Halifax. But, in addition, in November 1975 I had I bought a three hundred–acre farm in rural Nova Scotia. It was a rundown wreck that had been abandoned for fifteen years. With the help of many talented arti-sans, I spent hours, weeks, and months repairing and renewing the century-old eight-bedroom farmhouse. It needed new plumbing, new wiring, a new furnace and heating system, a new roof, new insulation and gyproc throughout, a complete paint job both inside and out, and furniture—because antique dealers and others had bro-ken in over the years and taken all the precious pine antiques. It was a labour of love for me. I had a bold vision of what it could become and a plan to make it happen. I had completed my dream kitchen of seven hundred square feet, with sixty-four handmade pine cabinets, built-in appliances, a floor-to-ceiling granite wood-burning fireplace, and two sinks. So by the time Linda and I were ready to marry, the big house was quite liveable, but not yet completed.

Linda and I decided we did not want a big wedding, but pre-ferred a small country event with close family. She came from a family of eight kids. We decided on a total of twenty-five people at the farm. It got a mention in the newspaper, and I clipped it out and saved it. Here's what it said:

A small, outdoor wedding took place on August 29, 1981, when Mary Linda MacLellan, daughter of Mildred and Duncan MacLellan of Halifax, was united in marriage with Donald H. Oliver, eldest son of Mrs. Helena and the late Clifford Oliver of Wolfville. The ceremony was performed by the Rev. Dr. W. P. Oliver of Lucasville, Halifax County. The soloist was Yvonne White, aunt of the groom.

Yvonne had a brilliant voice. I loved to hear her sing. She was a powerful mezzo-soprano. She was a frequent visitor to the farm, and when I had an upright organ there, my mother would often play and Yvonne would sing. I was so happy she could be part of the wedding. There were strong elements of Aunt Portia's greatness in Yvonne's voice, but as Yvonne was the youngest of thirteen children, her opportunities for support and guidance had been limited.

We had the usual wedding rehearsal and went through all the next day's procedures, from the vows to the rings. I felt prepared. Our wedding day brought sun and heat, with a slight afternoon breeze cooling the north lawn. We stood under a one hundred–year-old maple tree. My mother made an absolutely beautiful wedding dress for Linda. It was a fitted white Chinese silk dress with a blouson overdress, caplet sleeves, and a slit in each side of the overskirt. The waist was tied with a wide silk belt and bow.

Why that dress? I had spent twenty-one days touring China the year before. That had included a private audience with Deng Xiaoping, China's leader. He and I spent ninety minutes in the Great Hall of the People, where he told me about his four economic modernizations. I was captivated and thrilled. While I was in China I had time for a lot of shopping. I bought some elegant and beautiful Chinese fabric for my mother and sisters, and other presents for friends. For myself, I wanted to have five or six white silk shirts made that I could wear to my law office and other special places.

Back home a few months later, I went to look for my fabric and I could not find it. I made inquiries of Linda. We had talked about marriage, but had not set a date. Yet she was utterly confident in our future. She admitted she had seen the white silk fabric.

"The moment I saw it, I knew that you had secretly purchased it for my wedding dress," she said. I didn't tell her otherwise. So much for my elegant business shirts.

On the day of the wedding, my stepbrother, Reverend Oliver, oversaw our exchange of vows. Everything went smoothly, just as we had rehearsed. He took us through the wedding vows and said: "I now pronounce you husband and wife." Then he added: "Salute the bride."

I was stunned! We had not rehearsed that part. That word was nowhere in my notes. What was I supposed to do? My mind flashed to my high school days in the army cadets, where I had to salute almost every senior person who walked by me. I slowly started to raise my right hand to my brow. Linda, understanding exactly what was about to happen, quickly grabbed my arm and instead wrapped it around her waist. We embraced to the warm applause of our guests. It was a late start to a long, successful marriage of more than forty years.

We were a family from the start, as Linda brought her wonderful ten-year-old daughter, Carolynn Marie Oliver. I had known her since she was three. Her birthday was November 14 and mine was November 16, so there was instant bonding as two Scorpios. After Linda and I married, I adopted Carolynn and became the principal male influence in her life. Carolynn is a deeply ethical person, not so much out of any religious belief, but because she has an innate sense of warmth and kindness and respect toward others, and she does not want to see them harmed or taken advantage of. She has always had a group of moral principles that govern her behaviour or the way in which way she conducts herself with others. For instance,

Don's brother, the Reverend Dr. W. P. Oliver, conducted Don and Linda's marriage ceremony at the farm on August 29, 1981.

when she was young, I used to smoke and she complained on ethical grounds that it could potentially cause cancer or other illnesses to those in the same room or car. She warned me of the known dangers of second-hand smoke. I stopped smoking.

We used to live full-time in the city, but on weekends we enjoyed driving the ninety minutes to the farm. I thought for sure Carolynn would become a veterinarian, because she had so much warmth and affection for animals. When we had horses at the farm she loved riding and grooming them. In the summer, riding camp put her in seventh heaven. If a bird had an injured wing, she would want to find a way to have it repaired so the bird could fly again. She loved dogs, too. But there is another side of her: she is competitive and tenacious, in the sense that she never gives up and never stops trying. She can be very determined. These attributes were carried into school, sports, and all her extracurricular activities. And now they have been carried into her work and overall life.

Family life is extremely important to me. Regretfully, Linda and I did not have more children. I certainly would have loved to have had more, but we three very busy people managed to do many things together. Whenever possible, we would have two or three meals together a day; we would do something exciting together on a long weekend; we did sports together, particularly skiing, working out in a gym, or playing tennis or golf; we watched movies together, vacationed together, and where possible, worshipped together.

When we skied, Carolynn could easily keep up with me. One Christmas, on a family skiing vacation in St. Moritz in Switzerland when Carolynn was fifteen or sixteen years old, I was slowing down on a run near the bottom of the hill when I was hit from behind by a skier who was out of control. I was fine, except a contact lens was banged out of me. I searched in the white snow, which was gleaming from the sunlight, for the clear lens, but you can imagine how that went. Carolynn and Linda helped me search, but we gave up after twenty minutes. Carolynn agreed to ski with her "one-eyed dad" for the rest of the day. She had no problem speeding over the moguls with me.

I felt like I was quite a successful father, but one sad moment changed my thinking. I was extremely busy with trials in my law practice and needed every extra moment I could find to prepare. That meant spending holidays and weekends at the office. In addition, I volunteered in the Black community. I taught at universities. I was deeply engaged with business partners from Germany, and I often spent weekends in Munich for intensive meetings.

Carolynn was a star of her basketball team. She was the kind of athlete who, despite being on the verge of exhaustion, could muster the energy to make a mad dash for a mis-thrown ball, grab it, and, in the last ten seconds, score a basket and win the game for her team. One night over a family dinner she asked if I was flying off to Europe again for the weekend.

"I can't be sure, but I will know in a day or so," I said. "So, what's up"?

She looked me in the eye. "You are away too much," she said. "You are so busy, you're going to miss me growing up."

Well! I got that message loud and clear. That Saturday did not find me at a business meeting in one of the beer halls of Munich, but instead sitting next to Linda on a hard bench in a cold, dingy school gym watching young girls play basketball. My presence was noted.

❖

I had dreamed of being a diplomat, had tried my hand at journalism, and had finally settled on law. By 1990, I was fifty-two and comfortable in my life. But then I got a life-changing offer. Canada's Senate had vacancies in Nova Scotia and New Brunswick, and Prime Minister Brian Mulroney needed to fill them. A bill on abortion had faced certain difficulties in the House of Commons and was soon to reach the Senate. The prime minister would need a majority of Conservative supporters in the Senate to carry the bill. I knew all about the Senate from my legal and constitutional studies, but had never once thought about what senators actually did day by day, nor had I dreamed I would ever sit among them.

In the summer of 1990, I was working in my Halifax office when one of the firm's partners knocked on my door. He was well known as a Liberal, politically. "Did you see this?" he asked me. He showed me the *Toronto Star*, which had run an article listing potential candidates to fill the Atlantic Canadian Senate seats. To my surprise, my name and photo were among them. "They are thinking about *you* as a possible nominee for the vacant Senate seat in Nova Scotia!" he said.

I looked at my face in the newspaper. "No, I had not seen that," I told him. "That's a surprise. Maybe it's a trial balloon from the PMO."

I put it out of my mind.

A couple of months later I was in Toronto meeting with some potential investors from Japan to respond to an interest they had in the real estate project I was developing with my business partners from Germany. We were using one of the boardrooms at the accounting firm Deloitte. The negotiations were taking some time because most sentences had to be translated. In between the translations, the phone rang in the corner of the boardroom. I excused myself and answered. "Hello?"

"Is this Don Oliver?" the voice asked.

"Yes," I said, feeling a panic rising. Who would be calling me here and now?

"Where have you been? We have been trying to reach you for days. The prime minister wants to speak to you. Don't move from where you are," the voice instructed me. "Hang up now and in five minutes the phone will ring again. It will be the prime minister."

Well. I went to my Japanese colleagues and asked if they would kindly sit in the ante-room while I took a private call. I didn't mention it was the prime minister, but they agreed. Right at the appointed minute, the phone rang.

"Hello Donnie," came the instantly recognizable sonorous, warm voice of Brian Mulroney. "Donnie, how is your wife Linda? Is she still working in telecommunications? And is Carolynn still doing well in school?"

Donald Oliver was an active volunteer for the Progressive Conservative Party in Nova Scotia for many years. He is shown here serving as chair of the party's election committee in the 1970s.

I said yes to those questions and some others, and that seemed to give him some confidence that he was speaking with the right person. He spoke about how I'd joined the Progressive Conservative Party in the 1950s and had been a faithful, consistent volunteer for decades. He knew I'd been the chief legal director to several national electoral campaigns, that I had supported him for the leadership in 1976 and again in 1984, and that I had served for years on the executive of the PC Party both provincially and nationally.

"And over all those years as a volunteer without pay, no one really said thank you," he said. "You have also done a lot of work for your Black community as well, so I am now going to thank you by appointing you to the Senate of Canada."

I could open my mouth, but it produced no sounds. Thoughts flashed through my head as I processed this extraordinary conversation. *Could I do the job? Could I live up to his trust?*

I finally got my tongue moving. "Thank you, Prime Minister. Thank you very, very much. That is very generous. I am deeply honoured that you would do this," I said.

He must have noticed that I didn't actually accept the offer, as he explained that once I did, I would automatically be placed on the payroll and had only to go to Ottawa to be sworn in. He asked me to keep everything quiet until it was announced publicly the next Monday.

"Can I tell my wife and my mother?" I asked.

He said I could. Then the prime minister said he wanted me to return immediately to Nova Scotia and his office would provide a briefing about the announcement the next morning. My mind was in a frenzy as the call ended. So much to do! First, I had to figure out what to do with the Japanese businessmen in the next room. I needed to book a flight home. I needed to call Linda and my mother.

I will be forever thankful to the Right Honourable Brian Mulroney for having summoned me to the Senate of Canada on September 7, 1990. I promised him I would work hard at the job, and I did. Mulroney had many of the marks of greatness that I admire in people. He was a talented prime minister. He was not afraid to take bold stands. After a long, hard fight, he brought in the North American Free Trade Agreement, which brought Canada's economy into the modern age. We are a trading nation, after all! He was creative and clever in the ways in which he was able to implement major public policy change for the good of all Canadians, and in his private life he did so much to help people from all walks of life that he truly left his mark.

I was moved when he was the world leader who stood up for and worked strenuously for the release of Nelson Mandela from his apartheid prison in South Africa. On the international stage, he was the leader who managed to gently twist the arms of US president

Don and Linda Oliver in the Senate chamber on September 7, 1990, the day Don was sworn in to the Senate.

Ronald Reagan and British prime minister Margaret Thatcher to prompt them to support the efforts to free Mandela from prison. He was lauded as an international leader on climate change. He was ahead of the acid rain debate and will certainly go down as one of the finest prime ministers we have ever seen. I was so proud to be in his caucus and just to be on his team. I shall never forget his kindness. At the time, there was a long line of white aspirants to the Senate seat; lobbyists reminded him of that on a daily basis. The fact that he stood up for a Black man was remarkable.

But in some ways, it was as though my life came to an abrupt stop. Suddenly, I could no longer do many of the things I had been doing. I resigned from my law firm to avoid even an apparent conflict of interest with some of the major clients. I resigned, at great financial loss, from many business projects I had been actively engaged in. These are just a few of the things that made it a life-altering experience.

After I had been in the Senate for a few months, I and several other freshmen were sitting around having a drink when the question arose: "Where were you when you received your call from the Prime Minister's Office and were you expecting it?" We went around the room and I heard some absolutely fascinating stories about how some senators had nearly missed the telephone call. Others, with a hope and a prayer, had sat very close to the phone, waiting for it to ring. One person from Quebec had hired a private jet to get to Ottawa in time. Most interesting, indeed—a private jet!

When I first walked onto Parliament Hill in Ottawa, I saw little or no Black presence of significance in the House of Commons, the Senate, the Library of Parliament, or, most of all, in senior corridors of the Public Service, filtering down through every level of their departments. They certainly did not reflect the face or the mosaic of Canada. I discussed this with my seatmate, Senator Consiglio Di Nino, an Italian immigrant who lived in Toronto. He became a very good friend and was instrumental over the years in helping me set down a number of inquiries in the Senate to encourage debate on matters of anti-Black systemic racism.

Early on, I held a joint meeting with the chief librarian, the clerk of the Senate (the political version of a business CEO), and the clerk of the House of Commons. I told them bluntly what I observed and asked for their numbers on representation. They had none. I told them that the parliamentary precinct should be a place of joy, happiness, and harmony propelled by a clear understanding of the business case for diversity. Having people of different languages and cultural groups engaged together in the workplace really works. I realized that a major barrier to rooting out systemic anti-Black racism was a lack of hard statistics and data. Black people were not identified as a group that could be counted. When the government considered employment equity, it considered four specific groups: women, Indigenous people, disabled people, and visible minorities. The 1994 Employment Equity Act had no category for Black people; people of African descent. Instead, we were subsumed under the broad rubric of "visible minority," in which more than seventy-seven different nationalities and people could be included. That meant a large corporation or government could boast of having 30 percent of its employees from a visible minority without having a single Black person employed among the Chinese, Japanese, Korean, Thai, and Philippine people on their payroll. The other three target groups had made some modest progress, but Blacks were still at the back of the bus and at the bottom of the heap.

So it was with this massive bulwark that I had to negotiate and try to persuade the two parliamentary clerks and the lead librarian in Ottawa to be more representative of the four target groups. I started with the Senate. In the five previous years, there had been no visible minority hires into the Senate. None. All the table officers were white. All the committee clerks were white. It didn't reflect Canada. I made it the subject of one of my first Senate speeches. I laid out the current employee break-down and recited details of no new ethnic hires, and concluded by asking the administration to account to the Senate for why there were no people of colour, and specifically no Black people, hired in the last five years. I asked them if the problem was the availability of qualified talent, or if there were issues around having bilingual candidates, or if certain managerial skill sets were lacking. Exactly what was the reason Black people could have been overlooked for so long? I continued my work with the parliamentary agencies and the three hundred thousand members of the Public Service for the twenty-three years I was in the Senate. I was unrelenting in my task, and I now believe I made a difference.

The Senate empowered me to expand my campaign to expose many Canadians to the profound reality of white privilege and how it was the flip side of systemic anti-Black racism. It gave me new power to actively promote tolerance, equality, diversity, and fairness for all Canadians throughout both the public and the private sectors. I would use the power and resources of the Senate to build a business case for diversity.

Let me explain what I mean by "white privilege." It is an unearned benefit, like a perk, that is afforded to people based simply on the colour of their skin. That unearned benefit gives many white people countless social and economic advantages that people of other colours do not possess. This privilege is embedded deeply into the fabric and structure of our society. Many of the white senior officials I was to meet and work with were living day-to-day quite comfortably with what they have been taught about their unique privileges. I saw my job as a human rights activist and catalyst, challenging that mindset by encouraging people to explore some uncomfortable truths.

White privilege had been a focus of mine during my student years, and I wrote a lengthy article about it in the late 1960s. It ran with this introduction: "A new sense of dignity and self-worth is being felt and cultivated by Black men, as revealed in a challenging manner by Donald Oliver." In the article I asked,

> Why is one of the greatest achievements in our lives to be "accepted"—or tolerated—by white people who do not respect or tolerate our Black brothers and sisters? This question bites to the core of one's existence and essence. Once a Black man can accept that he is a slave today to his own inferiority complex, then and only then will he be capable of making a higher adjustment of claiming his equality.

I wrote that our generation felt that Black people were not inferior to white people or any other people. I wrote that, for years, the white man has had virtually all the social, political, and economic power that controls all our destinies. And now the Black man wants some power; some Black Power.

It has long been my view that there will always be racial strife as long as whites do not know the soul of the Black person. For too long, white people have been content with stereotypes. They must examine real Black lives. At the same time, white people must immediately begin an intensive process of self-examination. As Socrates said, "the unexamined life is not worth living." White people have a lot of examining of their own souls to do before they can ever understand anything about Black people.

White privilege is not overt racism. When a white person exercises their privilege, it is not necessarily an act of race hatred. No Black person would stare down a white person, saying, "I know you think you are great because of your privilege!" It doesn't work that way. It's innate. It's just there. It's been there for centuries. Many white people are oblivious to it, like when they get into an elevator and see a Black person and ask them to press their floor button. Why do you think I work in the elevator and not in the offices? It's easier and more comfortable for white people to take their assumptions for granted—an unconscious habit. It's extremely uncomfortable for them to recognize their privilege and start the examination. "Where did this come from? Why do I feel this way about Black people?"

So long as white privilege remains invisible, it will thrive. We must push it into the open and use it to start genuine dialogues. Even a little confrontation won't hurt. White people need to examine white privilege. When they go inside themselves and ask those uncomfortable questions, that's when these massive inquiries into the reasons for systemic anti-Black racism can come to an end. We must understand that the past is the past and everything that is white need not be intrinsically evil. To wrestle white privilege to the ground, we must work hand in hand to bring it out in the open—to expose it—to make certain it does not remain invisible.

❖

Nearly a decade passed and very little changed. In February 1998, I rose in the Senate to speak about the latest employment numbers for visible minorities. The report showed 3.2 million Canadians identified as a visible minority. I told the senators that the federal government's treasury board report on employment equity highlighted that no major initiatives had been set up to improve access to employment. Jean Chrétien's Liberal government sat on its hands. It did little to address the anti-Black systemic racism flowing throughout the entire public service.

In short, I pointed out to honourable senators that the government had taken ten years to increase visible minority representation in the workforce from 2 percent to 4.7 percent. And yet we represented about 10 percent of the country's population. Public servants are the face of government, I concluded, and all Canadians needed to see themselves reflected in the public service. Canada was broken; we must do something to fix it.

As Canada's first Black man to be appointed a senator (Anne Clare Cools had been the first Black Canadian named to the Senate, in 1984), I received many requests to give speeches, join panels, and take part in group discussions, especially during Black History Month. I spoke to schools, churches, universities—pretty much any group with a genuine interest in Black history. I wrote op-eds for newspapers. I preached tolerance, fairness, justice, and equality.

But in addition to taking a lead role in fighting anti-Black systemic racism in the Senate and other parliamentary institutions, I was very fortunate to play a major role in leading the debate on five critical pieces of legislation. After all, both the Senate of Canada and the House of Commons are primarily legislative bodies that study government and other bills in Committee and vote on them. The senate can be an effective tool for promoting good public policies, and the vast majority of senators, through their work across Canada, have proven former prime minister Pierre Trudeau wrong when he said of senators (who are Members of Parliament) that they are "nobodies fifty yards off the Hill."

I participated very actively in legislative matters in my twenty-three years in the senate. It began shortly after I was sworn in and the all-powerful Conservative leadership in the Senate wanted an experienced lawyer to chair the Committee on Transport and Communications in order to conduct a technical pre-study on a major piece of government legislation. I was asked and willingly accepted. Our mandate was to examine a proposed new Telecommunications Act. The Railway Act had governed Canada's telecommunications industry for eighty-seven years and it was obviously outdated. With relatively lower prices for telephone services in the United States in the 1990s, Canadian business and consumers had become more and more vocal about the need to introduce a more competitive telecom sector in Canada.

The bill was introduced for first reading but had not yet gone to committee in the House of Commons. I was given carte blanche by the minister, the Honourable Perrin Beatty, to have my committee do a thorough and comprehensive pre-study of the bill, and to make what amendments we deemed necessary to improve and strengthen the bill. We heard from fifty-five witnesses over many busy weeks of hearings. In the end, our committee recommended twenty-two major amendments to the telecommunications legislation. I wanted the new Act to be business-friendly, so instructed our researchers and writers to avoid regulation wherever possible; that is called the doctrine of forbearance. All twenty-two amendments passed in the House of Commons and became law. Al Gore, then the US vice-president, read our legislation and used it as a goal for his country. It ensured Canada could remain a world leader in telecommunications. After the bill became law, Ted Rogers, one of our witnesses and a telecommunications visionary, said how impressed he was at the way our Senate committee had been able to produce such a forward-looking piece of legislation.

The second piece of legislation was a private bill. For a completely different legislative turn, a chance conversation with my daughter had led me in an unexpected direction. One night after dinner I was working in my den when Carolynn popped by. "I'm off to a movie with a girlfriend and should be home around ten," she told me. "I just have to give her a buzz now to let her know I'm coming so she can phone the police."

My ears perked up. The police?

"What do the police have to do with a movie?" I asked.

Carolynn explained that her friend had been stalked and harassed for nearly two years by a terrifying man who left vile notes and dead squirrels and rats for her to find. He'd follow her when she went out, hiding behind trees and cars so he could get closer to her.

"There have been times she was in a grocery store shopping, picking something off a shelf, and he would be right there on the other side, peering through," Carolynn told me.

So her friend phoned the police every time she went outside. It didn't get her a police escort, but they would be nearby. It made her feel safer.

Stalkers seemed to be everywhere, and there appeared to be nothing that could stop them. I soon heard from other people dealing with similar harassment. One Sunday afternoon I was working at home; I was talking with a lawyer in Dartmouth to try to settle some of the cases we would contest against each other, or at least to narrow some of the issues to be proved in court. We had not finished our discussions.

"Oh! I've got to go now," he suddenly exclaimed. "My wife and daughter are out skating on the lake and the stalker might be there."

He hung up and our discussions were over.

I took the matter to the Senate. Stalking had become a federal crime in 1993, but the law proved to have limited effectiveness in prosecuting harassment and in protecting victims and potential victims. A Department of Justice study found 60 percent of criminal harassment charges were withdrawn or stayed, and that 75 percent of those convicted of criminal harassment only received probation or a suspended sentence. I spearheaded a push for tougher sentences for people found guilty of criminal harassment or stalking. I drafted and introduced a private member's bill in the Senate to triple the penalties for harassment and related offences, and to double the maximum penalty to ten years in prison.

I had strong support from the other side of the chamber, and once word of my bill got out, I received numerous letters, calls, and documents telling me about some of the frightening threats ordinary Canadians were receiving from stalkers. One woman phoned me from western Canada to thank me for my bill. She said in her case, the stalking, threats, and violence were so severe she was given a completely new identity, including a change of name, and moved far away to another jurisdiction so she could not be followed and threatened with more severe beatings, hate calls, and letters. "Mr. Oliver, with your bill I am feeling a sense of inner peace I have not had for years," she told me.

The justice minister at the time, Anne McLellan, set up a meeting with five of her senior political staffers in my office. She liked my bill a lot and wanted to include it in an upcoming omnibus piece of legislation. I willingly agreed. And so just like that, my idea became the law of the land. It told prosecutors, lawyers, and judges that the Parliament of Canada did not see criminal harassment/ stalking as a minor offence.

Five years later I took aim at spam email, especially spam that targeted children. Spam also hurt businesses, costing in productivity and adding to online security costs. I drafted a bill that would let people opt out of getting more emails from people, but it didn't pass. In 2004, I appeared before a federal task force on spam and made recommendations from my bill. That led to Canada's first anti-spam law in 2010. I was very pleased with that end result.

Next I drew up another private member's bill to have the Speaker of the Senate elected by secret ballot, not appointed by the prime minister. During the second reading debate in the Senate, I explained to senators that this bill did not require a constitutional amendment and that the House of Commons and the Senate alone could make the decision to have the Speaker elected by secret ballot. So, here's how that developed: in keeping with my long-standing interest in journalism, I continued to write op-ed pieces on public policy issues while in the Senate. In a recent one I had argued that we suffered from a democratic deficit in Canada and that the government should be more transparent, open, and accountable, and should be doing a lot more to engage Canadians in the political process. One evening, I was in my Senate office trying to catch up on some work and review plans for the next day when the phone rang. I checked the time: 7:00 P.M. I answered.

"Is this Don? It's Paul. Come to my office—I want to see you," he said.

That would be Paul Martin, the Liberal prime minister. I was surprised. I fumbled for a response.

"Which office are you in?" I blurted out.

"You know which one," he quickly replied. "Upstairs in the Centre Block."

I stood up, straightened my tie, put on my jacket and walked to his office. As my footsteps echoed off the halls, I wondered why he wanted to see me. I was a lifelong Conservative and he was a Liberal. In a bitterly partisan world, it was rare for one to ask to meet with the other.

After he welcomed me to his office and we exchanged some mutual greetings, he put a series of questions to me on democratic issues. He then mentioned the opinion piece on the democratic deficit and said he wanted to hear more. I told him I thought the prime minister could afford to give up certain powers.

"You know, sir, if you wanted to demonstrate to Canadians that you wanted to reduce your current democratic deficit, you could simply let the people speak through a vote," I told him. "You could consent to having an elected Speaker in the Senate chosen by secret ballot."

He listened. I reminded the prime minister that the House of Commons had an elected Speaker chosen by secret ballot and it was working well. He knew that the Speaker of the Senate was a powerful position. Under the current system, the prime minister appoints the leader of the government in the Senate, and sometimes they sit in cabinet, and he also appoints the Speaker of the Senate, who is fourth in the order of precedence. So when a prime minister with a majority in the House of Commons would appoint the leader and Speaker in the Senate, he would have absolute power over the entire Parliament of Canada, save for the elected Speaker in the Commons. When the meeting was finished, he walked me to the door and I couldn't help but add a last remark.

"You know, Prime Minister, I am aware that you did not answer my question about the elected Speaker," I said.

He paused a few seconds and with a little grin said to me, "You know, Don, that's the type of decision you make when you are leaving office!"

He never did make that change. The prime minister still appoints the Senate Speaker. My private member's bill did not pass.

The final piece of legislation that certainly deserves mention is Bill C-2, the Federal Accountability Act. In 2005, the year before Stephen Harper became prime minister, I had been doing some work and research on areas of government ethics and accountability. So I was extremely proud when the government asked me to chair the powerful Senate standing committee on legal and constitutional affairs. It was about to tackle what I believe was the largest bill ever brought before the Parliament of Canada. It amended more than sixty major statutes and brought about substantive changes to Canadian law, ensuring greater accountability, more transparency, and ethical government conduct.

What made it more challenging was that we were in a minority position in the Senate. C-2 would establish, for the first time, a legislative regime governing the ethical conduct of public office–holders, including cabinet ministers, ministers of state, and many other categories. It would create a new conflict-of-interest and ethics commissioner with more powers. In the Senate committee and in the chamber, the bill received more than 276 amendments, each of which had to be debated and voted upon. This all-embracing, powerful bill finally received third reading in the House of Commons and became law. It was an extraordinary exercise in bringing Canada's Parliament into the modern age and opening it up to public scrutiny. In the end I received a nice letter of thanks and a signed copy of the bill from the prime minister.

Chapter Nine

THE BUSINESS CASE FOR DIVERSITY

IN 2001, MY DEAR FRIEND LINCOLN ALEXANDER WAS approaching his eightieth birthday. I wanted to do something memorable and lasting to mark the day. As Black men, we both understood the fundamental importance of education in our lives and our society, and Lincoln had long been the chancellor at the University of Guelph, so I spoke with the president of Guelph, Alastair J. S. Summerlee, his vice-president of alumni affairs and development, Rob McLaughlin, and a few business associates and decided to initiate a special celebration to raise money for an educational cause close to my friend's heart. When word about our plan started to leak out, a lot of people in corporate Canada wanted to become involved to show their support for Linc. Ted Rogers was there, and Galen Weston kindly agreed to co-chair the event with me. (Galen Weston was one of Canada's most successful businessmen as chairman emeritus of George Weston Limited, a leading food processing and distribution company.)

I had the approval of the university and the finance group, but before proceeding further I arranged to have discussions with Linc. He was deeply honoured and said he wished the leadership gift to be directed toward a scholarship fund at the University of Guelph. I was in full agreement with that, so we developed a financial plan in which the high-value, prestigious award in Lincoln's name would be supported by an endowed fund; the goal was to raise between $800,000 and $1.2 million. I spent a lot of my time selling tables and collecting leadership gifts for the endowment. What we ultimately decided upon was to have two entrance scholarships, worth $5,000 each year for four years, totalling $20,000 per student. That would make it a most prestigious scholarship, which was precisely what we wanted.

We held a gala dinner to raise most of the money. Galen Weston made his corporate boardroom available to our planning team. Galen would attend meetings when he was available, and he always brought value to our discussions and our decisions. In our opening meeting he was incredibly gracious and kind to all of us. It was clear when he mentioned Linc that he held him in high regard and wanted this to be a great event to honour him. After weeks of intensive work by a team that grew to more than thirty volunteers, we were ready to go.

Before the gala took place, the *National Post* wrote: "Ontarians from all walks of life are preparing to honour a true statesman as he approaches his 80th birthday. His gentle presence has enriched public life and inspired thousands of young people—especially young Black people—to quest for the gold for more than half a century." The sold-out event was held at the Canadian Room at the

Royal York Hotel on December 13, 2001. I gave some opening remarks, welcoming everyone and thanking them for coming. I explained my relationship with Linc, and the use to which the funds from the evening would be put, and then the incredible show began, with videos, music, short speeches, and exciting foods that made your mouth water. Linda and I sat at the head table with Galen and his wife Hilary. It was an incredibly successful night in which we raised more than $600,000. In just one night we were well on our way to reaching our financial goal. It was soon met and surpassed, and the Lincoln Alexander Chancellor's Scholarship is among the university's most prestigious entrance awards.

Thanks to Galen's private generosity, there were tables set aside for Black youth so they, too, could attend and hear some of the untold stories behind the man and be inspired by his amazing achievements. It was a night of Blacks and whites pulling together as a team to pay tribute to a Black man who had made a difference for us all. It was a social event where people of all colours helped to show a quiet, peaceful way to strike at systemic anti-Black racism in Canada.

Lincoln sat on a number of corporate boards, and there were dozens and dozens of Canada's most senior corporate leaders at the gala. I thought, on hearing about Linc and all he contributed and accomplished, they were learning about Black Power and maybe, just maybe, some of these corporations could see the way clear to inviting some leading Blacks to take a seat on their board of directors, and also to fast-track some brilliant entry- or intermediate-level Black executives to senior vice-president positions. If those CEOs created diversity initiatives inside their corporations, that would seem to be the achievement of Black Power in Canada without the Black Panthers!

How is it possible to encourage white Canadians to close their eyes and consider some uncomfortable truths about the equality of women and men, irrespective of colour? As Lincoln wrote to me in a mentor's note: "It's about the myths and attitudes that exist by whites regarding people of colour." It was my hope that many of the senior gala guests could say, "Tonight we listened and we learned. We heard the messages about diversity and tolerance, and about how colour, particularly the colour Black, should not matter. Just look at the extraordinary life and contributions of Lincoln Alexander."

If through reason, persuasion, and experience, white privilege is removed, and if the business case for diversity takes its place, Canadians will be ready to demonstrate to the entire world just how well diversity can work. It would end systemic racism. In fact, I must note that throughout all my engagements in relation to the enormous undertaking of doing the gala dinner, at no time did I have to pause and remind myself that I was different from most other Canadians.

Wouldn't it be wonderful if forty or fifty of Canada's leading CEOs could take on a mentor role for a brilliant Black MBA, lawyer, or engineer in their company and teach them how to get into the succession stream? We would be extinguishing large amounts of white privilege in one blow. That is my dream. It brings out the goosebumps on me just thinking about it.

❖

A few years later, I was challenged to develop that idea during a meeting with a prominent bank president in Toronto. He'd invited me to lunch, and as a senator I was delighted to have the opportunity to discuss some financial aspects of current government priorities, as I understood them, with him. The view from his office's windows, thirty or forty storeys above the streets of Toronto, was stunning. As a staff member guided me through the executive level to the president's huge, impressive office, I took in the faces of the senior executives who were working intensely.

It was 2003. As a member of the powerful standing committee on banking, trade, and commerce in the Senate, I had had an opportunity to examine and cross-examine many senior finance officials across Canada. At times, they would invite committee members to private meals for a more personal conversation on business subjects, perhaps in the parliamentary restaurant. At this time the committee was studying principles of good corporate governance. We were considering compelling Canadian banks to create an arm's-length and independent chair of the board of directors, separate from the CEO. Often, they were the same person, and we didn't think that created the transparency and accountability necessary for such an important post. A lot of Bay Street people knew I was also a champion of diversity in the financial sector. Senator Leo Kolber, a long-time chair of the committee, mentions the effectiveness of our work in his memoir, *Leo: A Life.*

The bank president and I greeted each other and talked about the weather—always a rich subject in Canada. But I wanted to tell him as soon as I could about my observations just walking through the executive ranks of his bank.

"I saw many senior executive officers as I came to your office," I told him, "but no women, and no people of African descent."

He wasn't shaken.

"If they were talented and good, they would be working here, because the bank seeks out only the best," he said bluntly. He moved closer to me and raised his voice just a notch. "If you are suggesting that the bank discriminates against women and Blacks, then you are quite wrong."

He sat back a little and continued in a friendly but firm voice. "The bank, as a matter of internal policy, treats all people fairly and equitably," he said. "If you are suggesting we discriminate here against Black people, you're a lawyer: what's your proof?"

I tried to think of my response.

I was caught completely off guard. I had no proof, data, or statistics, legal or otherwise. All I had was just an opinion I'd formed walking to his office. He and I ended up having a successful lunch and had great discussions on new public policies in relation to the financial issues. We left our meeting on good terms.

Afterward, I turned his challenge over and over in my mind. It was a good question. What was my proof that his bank discriminated against women and Black people? Their mere absence from the executive floor was not evidence. He'd hit me in a soft spot. I knew of no such research. I realized that if I was going to make the business case for diversity in Canada really mean something, I needed proof.

Canada had legislation—the Employment Equity Act—designed in part to level the playing field for women, people with disabilities, Indigenous people, and of course the seventy-seven nationalities, plus Black Canadians, captured as "visible minorities." It was difficult to create legislation or programs for visible minorities as such, given the huge, diverse range of people it included, and that often stalled progress for Black Canadians.

I urgently needed a comprehensive, objective study that could withstand rigorous academic scrutiny from the most skeptical of opponents. I needed a non-political, highly respected think-tank with recognized, excellent researchers. I needed evidence that barriers kept Black people out of those jobs, and I needed this think-tank to create practical guides to removing the barriers. I settled on the Conference Board of Canada. It had a reputation for excellence and objectivity. I had several one-on-one meetings with Anne Golden, the CEO, and I made my needs for the comprehensive study known very clearly. She said they'd do it, but they couldn't pay for it. So I had to raise $500,000.

That figure sounded quite high to me, but I didn't want in any way to compromise the quality of the research. I desperately needed the objective data and statistics on anti-Black systemic racism and the extensive research that would accompany the data. All those public talks I'd given on tolerance, equality, diversity, and racism; all the panels I'd participated in; all the seminars where I had been a keynote speaker developing the business case for diversity—they'd helped me build up a potential network of possible donors.

The first name that came to mind was a connection I had with TD Bank. I had gotten to know the CEO over private lunches and at other events. For years, I'd been a judge on their panel selecting the youth winners of the prestigious TD Scholarships for Community Leadership. TD was keen to open the doors to diversity and used the award to help students who did great work in their communities and got excellent grades, too. I met the most inspiring people and heard incredible stories of creative community projects. I called my friend Scott Mullin, a senior vice-president at the bank. I told him about the research project I was proposing and what it would cost, and asked if TD would help. They wrote a cheque for $50,000 the next week. Jim Judd, secretary of the treasury board, with whom I had worked on these issues, put in another $50,000. And with that first $100,000 in hand, I worked my connections at BMO Financial Group, BCE Inc. (formerly Bell Canada Enterprises), George Weston Limited, Power Corporation of Canada, Sun Life Financial, and several others. At BMO, for instance, vice-president Paul Deegan, a long-time friend, was very helpful in encouraging the bank's contribution.

I'm sure they all knew about the November 2000 Coca-Cola case in the US, where years of racial discrimination against Black employees had led to a landmark $193 million settlement. Texaco had paid $176 million for similar anti-Black racism. I had given a major speech in the Senate on those cases, noting how we had similar oppressive and racist practices in our own corporations. So contributing to a $500,000 project to research discrimination in Canada probably seemed like a good investment, if it would help them fix the problems without class-action lawsuits. I soon had the money. I paid the Conference Board of Canada after ensuring I would chair an oversight committee to which the researchers would regularly report.

Early on I noticed the conference board researchers were timid in their language characterizing what they observed and learned. Careful observation revealed the board members were reluctant to use the word "racism." I was glad I was there with the strong support of people like Sharon Ross to help get them back on track. Sharon Ross was one of the driving forces behind the Black Cultural Centre, and she asked some very tough but important questions. In the end, the researchers produced the most detailed and comprehensive research report ever produced in Canada on systemic barriers to advancement for visible minorities in the public and private sectors.

We produced an action guide, called *Business Critical: Maximizing the Talents of Visible Minorities*. It proved popular, and it worked. Part of it was an employment systems review, which got companies to do a comprehensive examination of their organizations' policies, programs, and practices with the goal of identifying and removing systemic and attitudinal barriers. Next, it advised companies on how to recruit or attract Black people and other visible minorities. It analyzed how systemic racism can affect interviews for jobs through inherent biases people often have. In short, this Conference Board study proved that there was racism, anti-Black systemic racism, at the heart of promotions and advancement in both the public and the private sectors in Canada. With the help of experienced researchers who produced statistics, data, and case studies, in addition to other proof, the business case that diversity works was clearly set out. The report concluded that "valuing diversity goes beyond business necessity to business survival itself."

So what are the key things I drew from the Conference Board study that I funded? First there is proof that anti-Black systemic racism, and racism against visible minorities in general, exists in both the public and private sectors in Canada. Secondly, and even more importantly, diversity works. The classic definition of diversity is that it is the practice or quality of including or involving people from a range of different social and ethnic backgrounds, and of different genders and sexual orientations, and speaking many different languages, and so on. The business case for diversity to me means that the acceptance of these differences pays huge dividends and makes the world a better place. The key is to accept these differences and look to the enhancements in the bottom line. This is the takeaway I gave in all my lectures in Norway, Denmark, Sweden, Brazil, Geneva, and London: diversity works. Diverse companies are more likely to outperform less diverse peers on profitability. That's because diverse corporations have higher profits and greater revenue to the bottom line, where they could increase dividends, should the board of directors so decide. Diverse corporations have less turnover and have much more positive corporate cultures. That's the essence of the business case for diversity that I spoke about constantly in my twenty-three years in the Senate of Canada, and on into my retirement.

It turned out a lot of people and corporations were looking for just the kind of comprehensive business guide for diversity that our well-researched Conference Board study provided. I was flooded with invitations to speak about it around the world. Human-resource managers across corporate Canada and in the senior ranks of the public service used it as a guide to develop their own policies and practices. Many of our largest banks and financial institutions used large portions of the practical guides. The goal was to drive diversity into the core of the companies to let them fully capitalize on the talents of their Black employees.

The Conference Board report generated invitations for me to speak in countries all over the world. On the Scandinavian wing of the tour, I spoke in Norway, Sweden, and at Aarhus University in Denmark, where I began by speaking about Canada's multicultural framework as a possible model for integrating racial and ethnic minorities in Scandinavia. From there I moved to the business case for diversity and its essential importance in society. I explained how inclusion and tolerance go hand in hand with the making of the business case. In an open debate after my lecture, one participant told the assembly that Denmark didn't want to become a multicultural society, but it was slowly becoming a multi-ethnic one. Many Danes didn't want that. I was told that, unlike Canada, Denmark had for centuries been a homogenous white nation with one language and one religion. One speaker told me that, with their long-established tradition of homogeneity, they had a hard time extending rights and privileges to "people who don't look like us." That obviously included people who looked like me. In one part of Scandinavia, an immigrant would have to live and work there for nine years before even being eligible for consideration for some type of permanent status. And there I was preaching: "Learn how to accept difference! Diversity works." The Conference Board report was very helpful.

After Denmark, I made some slight alterations to my speeches and interventions in Norway and Sweden. Throughout Scandinavia, the question was: "How can we keep what we have without giving it all up to new immigrants?" I began by saying that Canada didn't start with a debate on multiculturalism, but rather the country was born from our Indigenous peoples and that the French and English later brought two new cultures, languages, systems of law, religions, and ways of life. We in Canada had learned to live with the interweaving of these various cultures into our national fabric.

I told my mostly white northern European audiences that Canada had long ago realized that this diversity gave our country certain advantages. It made us a more interesting country to live in—and in learning to live with our many languages and cultures, it was not difficult to take the third step of embracing immigrants and other visible minorities.

In 2008, the Norwegian government had made it mandatory that women comprise 40 percent of all boardroom members on listed private companies. In Norway, I often spoke at business meetings where women outnumbered men two to one. Norway was a world leader in gender equality and could teach Canada how to do it.

In Malmö, Sweden, in a beautiful building near Gustav Adolfs Torg (Square), I received dozens of questions about Canadian multiculturalism and immigration. What did it mean? How did it work? Did people accept it? Everywhere I went, the Conference Board of Canada report went. Many people studied it to improve their own countries. But it wasn't all work. I even got to attend the world-famous Royal Swedish Opera for a powerful performance of Puccini's *Tosca*. The acoustics were incredible. Tears came to my eyes and goosebumps to my flesh when Tosca ran to the parapet and flung herself to an artistic "death" at the end of the third act.

When I returned to Canada, I was pleased with how well the report had worked. The only question remaining was: would Canada embrace it? I certainly looked forward to the next time a sharp-minded CEO asked me to show him the evidence for the business case for diversity. Yes, anti-Black racism and white privilege exist, and yes, there are many things the public and private sector can do to dismantle them.

The report was good for me personally. It had been created because I had been appointed a senator to attempt to make good things happen in Canada. It took away the constant reminder that I'm different from most Canadians and that somehow, I must prove that I am worthy to participate in and enjoy all the fruits that have been bestowed on the white majority because of white privilege. I had proved it. I could now enjoy it.

Chapter Ten

RETURN TO
AFRICA

AN HONORARY DEGREE FROM A CANADIAN UNIVERSITY IS indeed an incredible honour and is something any recipient should be very proud of.

I am humbled to have been conferred with honorary doctoral degrees from York University, Saint Mary's University, Acadia University, and Dalhousie University. But as I look back over my life, the one most special to me was the honorary degree from the University of Guelph. My dear friend Linc Alexander, as chancellor of Guelph, presided over the 2006 convocation ceremony and conferred on me the degree of Doctor of Laws, honoris causa. It was a profoundly moving and cherished occasion for me. My mentor and I sat side by side in the auditorium, and after I delivered the convocation address to the graduating students, Linc congratulated me. It was a very special moment for me.

In 2006, Senator Donald Oliver received an honorary Doctor of Laws from the University of Guelph. Senator Oliver described the moment as "profoundly moving" because his dear friend Lincoln Alexander, then chancellor of the university, conferred the degree upon him.

I continued to sit next to him on the stage for more than two hours while hundreds of students received their diplomas, and he said many more powerful things about me and my career, and encouraged me to keep up the struggle. He told me to not give up the fight and to continue to be a catalyst for tolerance, diversity, and positive change when it comes to defeating anti-Black systemic racism. It was an awesome and powerful day for me and there were times I had difficulty holding back tears of joy.

I observed one of the most amazing things about Linc. He took a personal interest in every student who walked across the stage. He had a word for everyone. He didn't just nod as they went by. Sometimes, having read their degree and hometown on the program, he might say, holding a student's hand: "Well, Mary, congratulations on getting your bachelor's degree in science. I'm sure the people back home in Chardville will be equally proud of you. Just keep up your hard work and I'm sure things will continue to go well." Or he might say: "Well, you've got the degree, what are you going to do next"? He carried on a brief conversation with each of them. At the reception after the ceremony many of the students could be heard asking: "What did he say to you?" and "He is such a nice man." It was really quite incredible. He had charisma and a unique charm that was infectious.

❧

In 2008, I returned to Africa. It had been forty-seven years since my summer in Ethiopia and things had changed. I found it a country teeming with economic activity and vitality. It was like coming home again. Ethiopians had thrown off the shackles of a restrictive military regime and built an economy generating record growth, even amid the global recession. Ethiopia's growth in the last few years exceeded that of any other country in Africa. The entrepreneurial spirit was everywhere: with children, women's groups, local associations, university campuses—all the way up to the government of the land. I was delighted to be among Ethiopians again. They are wonderful, caring, generous, warm, and considerate, and most of all, fun people to be around.

I'd kept some ties while I was away, working with a professional group of Ethiopian-Canadians in Ottawa who helped support higher academic institutions in their homeland. The group is called AHEAD, the Association for Higher Education and Development. It had begun in 1989 to help medical students who had the academic talent to succeed, but not the money. Those bright students often couldn't buy shoes, clothes, food, or transportation, let alone books and medical supplies. Linda and I donated money, and I then persuaded Senator Wilbert Keon, a retired leading Canadian heart surgeon, to give his entire medical library to one of the top medical schools we were supporting in Addis.

Senator Donald Oliver persuaded Senator Wilbert Keon, a retired Canadian heart surgeon, to donate his entire medical library to one of the top medical schools in Addis Ababa, Ethiopia.

We managed to supply all the basic medical supplies in the four schools we supported, plus money to provide necessities for dozens and dozens of students, many of whom have now graduated and are serving the needs of Ethiopians throughout the country. Several of them are now working in remote areas where there had never been a medical doctor. I became an honorary patron of AHEAD in Canada. While in Addis, I met with a number of AHEAD-affiliated officials.

As I prepared to give a talk on managing diversity at the symposium I was attending, my thoughts floated back over the half-century to my summer in Maimisham, where the shy locals had taught me how deep diversity can be a strength. It was to be a routine lecture, but that changed when I met the other panellists. One was John Packer, the well-known director of the Human Rights Centre at the University of Essex. The other panellist introduced herself as Mrs. Netsanet Asfaw, a Member of Parliament from Tigray province—she represented the people I had spent the summer with in 1962. Amazingly, it was her late uncle who had invited us to come. She remembered the school project well and told me it was still in active use.

"People still ask me, 'I wonder whatever happened to those people from afar who came here to build our school?'" she told me. Now she could tell them. She and I had a wonderful reminiscence about the people of her home and my time there. We had helped to make a positive difference.

I was able to help make a positive difference in Canada in 2008. MP Jean Augustine (she had been elected the first Black female Member of Parliament in 1993 and was appointed the first Black woman in Cabinet in 2002) had brought a motion before the House of Commons to have February recognized as Black History Month. She handled it in the House of Commons and I brought it to the Senate, the upper house of government. Nothing could happen without the Senate's approval. So in order for Canadians to know that the Parliament of Canada fully supported February as Black History Month, I drew up a motion. It read: "To recognize the contributions of Black Canadians and February as Black History Month." I tabled the motion with the clerk, and it was put on the orders of the day for March 4, 2008. I did not know if it would pass or not, although I had lobbied a number of senators, soliciting their support. When the Speaker called the item on the order paper and asked for the vote, it passed unanimously. I had completed Canada's parliamentary position on Black History Month. I was absolutely delighted. It was one of my proudest days in the Senate. It was now official.

❖

In 2008, I returned to Africa once again. I flew from Ottawa to Cape Town, South Africa, where I led the Canadian delegation at the 118th assembly of the Inter-Parliamentary Union, or IPU.

Senator Donald Oliver with Prime Minister Stephen Harper during one of their many long chats about diversity.

The theme was "Pushing Back the Frontiers of Poverty." I spoke about Canada's efforts to reduce poverty and how Prime Minister Stephen Harper had guided Canada's "Save a Million Lives" initiative to double Canadian assistance to Africa over the last few years.

I fell in love with Cape Town's old-world charms amid the spectacular beauty of the point where the Atlantic and Indian Oceans meet. Or at least that's what the tourist propaganda told me. The oceans actually meet at Cape Agulhas, which is the southernmost part of Africa, but that doesn't sound as mysterious and enchanting. But I went with the myth and stood on Table Mountain and pretended I was watching the cold Atlantic water caressing the warmer water of the Indian Ocean. It's fun to let it all hang out and just dream sometimes!

Cape Town was a vibrant, colourful mix of old European charms and African culture. I loved dining out at their exquisite restaurants, an oasis of calm amid the bustling streets. Their excellent South African wines go so well with a lot of the indigenous foods and it was fun to sample their vast array of great restaurants.

The Canadian delegation made a number of significant interventions at the conference that put our policies on the record. We debated human rights violations in the recent election in Zimbabwe. Unfortunately, it was necessary for me to leave Cape Town in a hurry, indeed, even before the conference's closing ceremony, because I'd received an urgent request from the Department of Foreign Affairs and International Trade in Ottawa to represent Canada by attending a meeting of heads of state at the Southern African Development Community Conference (SADC) in Mauritius.

Well, I'd never been to beautiful Mauritius before. It was another African hidden gem, a jewel in the Indian Ocean. Flying into that enchanting island reminded me a lot of Barbados. I was arriving in a country with a quiet, charming countryside, with some farms still producing sugar cane. The narrow, winding roads, the terrain, and the cane were all so Barbadian, it seemed. I also saw beautiful white sandy beaches, with tall palm trees swaying back and forth, as though inviting me to come over and get refreshed. Mauritius is a volcanic island of beautiful lagoons with coral reefs surrounding most of the coastline. Nowhere did I see any sign of poverty or strife. I knew I had come to work, but it was so enchanting and refreshing.

I was joined there by the Canadian ambassador to Zimbabwe, Roxanne Dubé. It was a truly fascinating experience. We mingled with some of the most powerful, eloquent, and intelligent leaders in Africa. We lobbied the presidents and prime ministers about Canada's public policies on Zimbabwe. Zimbabwe had held elections in March 2008 that led to a presidential runoff that had created a tense situation of increasing violence. The SADC was leading a political dialogue to resolve the issue. The SADC's chair, Thabo Mbeki, was our main contact point. He was also the president of South Africa, succeeding Nelson Mandela in that role.

The Canadian position on the Zimbabwe elections had been printed and circulated, so all the heads of state were familiar with where we stood. Robert Mugabe, who had fought for Black independence from Great Britain, had become prime minister in 1980 and was still in power in 2008. He ran an authoritarian regime responsible for widespread human rights abuses and violations. Zimbabwe was once the "breadbasket" of Africa, but no longer.

Looking at the makeup of the SADC countries that also border Zimbabwe, I could begin to appreciate how difficult our Canadian lobbying was going to be. Botswana, Zambia, Mozambique, and Swaziland (now eSwatini) were all neighbours. Namibia, Malawi, and Lesotho weren't that far away either. They were a close fraternity and would find it hard to speak out publicly and meaningfully against the human rights and electoral rights violations at the hands of Mugabe.

In quiet Port Louis, Mauritius, Ambassador Dubé and I began our work. We attended numerous bilateral meetings with foreign ministers and heads of state. Having just come from Cape Town at the IPU Conference where the elections in Zimbabwe had been discussed and debated, whenever I had the opportunity, I referred in my meetings with leaders to a statement from the 135 national parliaments that expressed their concerns regarding the facts that the detailed results of the presidential elections had not been released even after the passage of several weeks. I repeated the IPU message: "The people of Zimbabwe have a right to determine their future through free and fair elections." That was clearly our Canadian message. But it did not take me long to realize the reluctance of the SADC leaders to say anything against Mugabe's Zimbabwe.

I had met President Mbeki once before and found him decisive, clear, quite sophisticated, and interesting. Educated in the UK, with a master's degree in economics from Sussex University, he had been influenced by many intellectuals while there and developed a keen interest in writers and poets like Brecht, Shakespeare, and Yeats. I passed him in a hallway and mentioned we had met before. We spoke of Canada and South Africa's long, good relationship, especially due to the work of former prime minister Brian Mulroney.

"I am well aware of Canada's help and to the work of Mulroney," he replied.

I asked him if we could spend ten minutes together to discuss Canadian policy on Zimbabwe. He said nothing, turned on his heel, and walked off without looking back. I was undaunted. From then on, when I saw him at one of the meetings, I would walk slowly toward him and look to get a word into the conversation. Each time he saw me, he would drop eye contact, turn, and walk away. I persisted. Finally, in one of the last meetings on the schedule, I cornered him. He turned and pointed his finger at me.

"I don't want to talk with you," he said. "Mugabe is my friend."

Well, we might have achieved 90 percent of Canada's goals for the mission, but it looked like we wouldn't fully win this one. It made me glad I hadn't followed my childhood dream of becoming an international diplomat!

Chapter Eleven

PUTTING POLICY INTO ACTION

ALL THE POLITICAL PARTIES IN CANADA'S PARLIAMENT HAVE a private, family-type caucus meeting each Wednesday morning to discuss political and strategic issues. Early in the fall of 2009, after one of our morning Conservative Party caucuses, Prime Minister Harper was leaving the room, shaking hands and having a word with various members of the House of Commons and senators. As he passed by where I was standing, he looked over in my direction, smiled, and said, "Give me a call." And then he left.

I was not sure if he was serious or just letting me know that if I had serious issues that I would have his ear. Was it "give me a call sometime," or "give me a call today"? He was in good spirits, so I thought he was just being nice and friendly. It certainly made me feel good to be singled out like that. We had had several one-on-one talks before on a variety of public policy issues. But I did not want to be imposing or bother his staff by trying to set up a meeting that I was not sure was a meeting, so I was quite reluctant and somewhat nervous to phone. The upshot was that I did not phone. I decided to put the matter to the back of my mind and went about my work.

A few days later, the phone in my Senate office rang and it was the PMO; the voice on the line said, "the prime minister would like to speak with you." I then heard the prime minister himself. "I thought I asked you to phone me," he said right off the top. He did not sound too pleased to be chasing me, or maybe that was just my imagination. But it only took seconds for his good humour to come out.

"I have to go to Washington next week to have a bilateral with President Obama in preparation for the next G20 summit in Pittsburgh, and I want you to come along," he said. "I have made arrangements for you to meet the president. I have told him about the work you have been doing in the Black communities that mirrors some of the things he did in Chicago. My office will give you the details of the flight." I could hardly speak, but managed to say, "Thank you for this great honour, sir," before we ended the call.

Wow! Such a meeting seemed so remote that I hadn't even dreamed about it yet. I put down the phone, feeling dizzy. I would meet the first Black president of the United States, and meet him in the White House. I felt dazed. I put my elbows on my desk with my head in my hands and just said, quietly, "Thank you." I was feeling so lucky and so fortunate and so blessed.

My inbox was flooded with emails from the PMO, detailing every moment of the coming journey. Our itinerary was for September 15, 16, and 17, 2009—the days leading up to the G20.

I thought about what to pack. What should I wear to meet Barack Obama? I thought about my black suit, but felt it would not present me as being happy about meeting him. Grey? Too solemn. I settled on my blue pinstriped suit with a contrasting red silk tie. I packed my bag, made all the necessary cancellations at home, and was ready. It would be wheels-up in the prime minister's Challenger jet at Hangar 11 at 16:15. I arrived at the Canadian Reception Centre at the Ottawa MacDonald-Cartier International Airport early, went through the security protocols, and was seated in the reception area. As departure time approached, I boarded and took my assigned seat on the jet that also had a number of other people, including the prime minister's personal security RCMP team, plus some key PMO advisers.

I relaxed and unwound in the comfortable seats. About ten to fifteen minutes before landing, one of the RCMP officers came back to me and said they had just learned there was a security issue. My heart began to pound. What big security issue could prevent us from landing? What was happening down there? But I was quickly relieved of all anxiety when he had a chance to explain that we just had to circle a bit because Air Force One was coming in at the same time, and as a security protocol it had priority to land ahead of us. I got a look at it as it landed. It's a big plane. Our jet suddenly seemed rather small. As I watched from our slowly circling plane, I could see the president quickly leave his behemoth and step to a waiting helicopter. He was whisked back into the air and a second helicopter, packed with armed security personnel, followed the president from Andrews Air Force Base.

We touched down, were met by some embassy staff, and proceeded to the Mandarin Oriental Hotel. I had a nice room and stayed in it for a light dinner. I went to bed early, my mind racing through scenarios. I tried to plan the day. I pictured President Obama walking toward me, that famous smile and easy manner, extending his hand to me. What should I say first? How could I make a good impression? I had been told that the PMO had briefed the president on the work my family had done for the Black community over the last century. I shouldn't repeat that, I thought.

I drifted off to sleep, running through opening lines. I woke up still buzzing with excitement. I re-read the itinerary to check again whether I was missing anything, but no. I was ready. I put on my blue pinstriped suit and red silk tie and went down to the lobby at 9:30 A.M. We were due to meet the president in the White House at 10:45 A.M. We piled into our vehicles and drove to 1600 Pennsylvania Avenue. We went through a series of stringent security measures, even though we were part of the prime minister of Canada's delegation. Security first. No exceptions.

Prime Minister Harper was told the president was running a few minutes late, so we stood outside the Oval Office. I took in everything. It hardly seemed possible I was in the real White House, about to meet the actual president of the United States. Security asked for my phone and any other electronic equipment. We all had to hand over our devices before entering the inner sanctum. A senior aide finally turned to the prime minister. "You may enter now, sir." A door to the left opened, revealing President Obama.

"Welcome to the White House," he said, shaking the prime minister's hand. "Come in." A staff photographer captured each handshake. We entered the famous Oval Office. I cleared my eyes, looked up and around the room. It felt like the centre of the world. The room represented the ultimate place of power and influence in our world. President Obama was the most powerful person in that world. So many critical historical events had happened right in this space. And here I was. It took my breath away. Everything was meticulously appointed, from the carpets to the paintings on the walls to all the furniture.

The Oval Office was smaller than I thought it would be. Behind the iconic presidential desk stand three big windows, with another window to the left of centre. A fireplace sits at the front of the room and four doors connect it to the rest of the White House. The Rose Garden, where I had witnessed President Kennedy speak a lifetime before, was just outside the window. The office itself was about ten metres long and eight metres wide.

A few US cabinet members arrived for the meeting. The first was Hillary Clinton, the secretary of state. I happened to know her, so I went over and we had a nice chat. I reminded her that I had been present when she'd received an honorary degree from Mount Saint Vincent University in Halifax, and that she had given a brilliant speech on the challenges of modern education. She smiled warmly in recalling the event. She was easy to talk with, as one would expect from such a seasoned politician.

President Obama chaired the meeting. He was clearly thoroughly briefed on all the issues, yet appeared relaxed; almost nonchalant. He seemed happy to see his Canadian guests. He did not appear to have a structured agenda, nor a pre-established set of targets to talk about to declare the meeting a success. Instead, he seemed ready and willing to roll with the punches and just see where the discussions led. He knew, of course, that our prime minister also had a brilliant mind and had a lot to contribute to move the yardsticks forward. Their discussions had been planned to focus on economic recovery measures and initiatives, and energy security and progress under the US–Canada Clean Energy Dialogue. They would also discuss the key issues likely to surface before the Copenhagen summit.

Everyone in the room hung on every single word the president uttered. He could be witty, and because he seemed so comfortable with his Canadian allies and friends, he showed us a lot of warmth. He charmed us easily. I was fascinated by the interaction between Hillary Clinton and the president. They had run against one another and there had been times during that election campaign that the pressure had gotten pretty high. Now they were working as a well-functioning team in which they supported one another. They were both highly intelligent, very quick, and very politically astute. And when it came time to find ways for Canada to become involved, they pulled together like a well-trained team. Our prime minister laid out our key Canadian concerns about trade irritants. The leaders covered a lot of exciting topics and then they wrapped it up.

"It's now time for the media to come in," the president said. "I want everyone else to move back—way back, because when they come in with their big cameras, they could easily hit and injure one of you."

He wasn't joking. I moved back. The door opened. The journalists poured inside, lugging cables, wires, boom mics, and heavy cameras. The photographers took photos of the two leaders' feet, legs, backs, fronts, faces, suits—everything. I slid further back in the room, trying to stay out of the way, but I guess I went too far back. I leaned over and put my bag on a table and one of the presidential staff came running after me. "Take your bag off that desk!" they said sternly. I quickly removed my bag, feeling a little embarrassed. What could I do wrong next? I wondered, anxiety churning my stomach. I took another look at the desk and realized it was the Resolute desk, which had been built from the oak timbers of the Arctic exploration ship, HMS *Resolute*, and had been a gift from Queen Victoria. Presidents Kennedy, Carter, Reagan, Clinton, George W. Bush, and now Obama, had used it. President Kennedy's son had famously played under it during his father's tenure. The desk's history dated back to 1880 and it was a priceless historical artifact—and I had used it to stash my bag! I stepped away from the desk.

I noticed the communications people had ushered the last of the media out of the room. "Senator, do you want to come up now?" a voice asked me. That was my cue. My heart pounded. I was in awe of the Oval Office and scared to death to actually meet President Obama. He smiled at me and said some very flattering things that he had learned about my career, my contributions to the Black community, and my work on diversity. I prayed his staff hadn't told him I'd also used the Resolute desk as a storage area. I found my voice and mentioned his community-organizing work in Chicago and the importance of giving back. We talked about racism in our two countries. I felt so uptight and nervous. I was amazed sensible words kept flowing out of my mouth.

Standing by the window, I was suddenly transported to a very different world. I thought not of power and pomp, but of poverty and chains. "Do you know, sir," I said to the president, "not far from here, in Virginia, my maternal grandfather was born in a family of slaves, got his freedom, and came to Canada. I, his grandson, was the first Black man in history to be summoned to the Senate of Canada."

This office had once been the centre of my family's oppression. Now I stood inside it, with the prime minister of Canada, meeting the president of the United States. Imagine if my ancestors could have glimpsed this day from their captivity.

"Well," President Obama said, "let's have a photo of our two firsts—you as the first Black man to be a senator, and me as the first Black president of the United States."

He called the photographer over. We posed and the camera snapped. Just the two of us. As though my head was not big enough already, he added, "How would you like to have your photo taken standing between the prime minister of Canada and the president of the United States?"

"I will be deeply honoured, sir," I answered. Prime Minister Harper joined us and it was done. The resulting photo shows me beaming, excited, and so very proud. If only my parents could see me now, I thought. And my grandparents, and my great-grandparents. They, too, would be so proud. What a day. What a memory. What a moment. We soon were escorted out of the Oval Office and the White House.

That evening, I was invited to join the prime minister and a small group for dinner at a cozy restaurant downtown. I had no idea how much security we had covering our dinner party until I stood up and started walking toward the washroom. Several people suddenly stood up, and one of them actually escorted me to and from the room.

The next day, the prime minister invited me to join in his morning briefing with the Ottawa office, which I found very interesting. Later that day we met with Speaker of the House Nancy Pelosi, Senator Harry Reid, Senate Majority Leader Mitch McConnell, and other well-known senators including Chuck Grassley, Susan Collins, Bernie Sanders, and Amy Klobuchar. It was another awe-striking day. There were other interesting activities on the trip, but the main event was over and it was time for me to pack my bag, gather up the memories of all my incredible experiences, and head back to Canada.

❖

Throughout my time in the Senate, I did my best to awaken Canadians to the reality of anti-Black systemic racism. Sometimes that was through writing. Sometimes the headlines on those pieces frightened people, as did the title of a 1991 op-ed in the journal *Spectrum*: "Strong Forces Bar Black Canadians," a 2011 Postmedia piece: "Senator Urges Blacks to 'Rise Up and Claim Our Rightful Place,'" and "It's Time to End White Privilege and White Supremacy in Canada" in the *Globe and Mail* in 2020.

Speaking out in the public forum was one part of the work; another was speaking truth to power behind closed doors. Over my career in the Senate, I maintained a good working relationship with the community of deputy ministers. Deputy ministers are the senior civil servants who carry out the will of the government. Twice, I spoke at the private deputy ministers' breakfast, which was held weekly around an oval table in the former Langevin Block, now known as the Office of the Prime Minister and Privy Council building on Parliament Hill. The building was opened in 1889 and is a majestic piece of architecture that faces the Parliament buildings on Wellington Street. More than forty of the most senior deputy ministers of Canada sat around the table for the meeting, which was chaired by the clerk of the Privy Council.

It was a distinct honour for me to be invited to the clerk's meetings with senior deputy ministers. It was unique and I was frankly very privileged. But it also saddened me, because when I looked around the oval table, I saw a sea of white faces. Where was the Canadian mosaic I saw walking down the main streets of our big cities?

In my first appearance, I gave extensive data and statistics to prove that diversity works. I told them about my sister Eugenie, who had the highest academic marks in grade eleven but who had been bypassed for the gold medal by the school administration because of the colour of her skin; she had received the silver medal instead. I also told them about some of my own personal academic encounters with anti-Black systemic racism. I'd barely left the room when my inbox started filling up with emails from deputy ministers who said they had been moved by my talk, and who wanted to meet and learn what they could do in their own departments to root out the layers of systemic racism that were impeding bureaucratic progress. They wanted their offices to reflect the faces of Canadians.

I also spoke to the deputy ministers, as a guest presenter, during private working policy retreats that took place away from Parliament Hill. I talked about diversity and emerging public policy initiatives in which race should be considered. I told them that diversity broadens the idea pool and brings new problem-solvers to the table. Visionary, committed leadership is crucial. I strongly encouraged them to reinforce among managers that complacency about racism is not an option. I told them not to ignore racist remarks and hope that they will go away and that, as a better way to nurture a culture of inclusion, they should challenge employees if they encounter racism. Sometimes you could hear a pin drop when I was speaking—and I took that as a sign I had their full attention.

In one address I gave, called "Achieving Greatness through Diversity and Inclusion," I told the senior bureaucrats that diversity is just having a mix of peoples and cultures in a society; inclusion is what makes the mix work. I said that in order to succeed, each deputy minister must build pathways to inclusion and tolerance for Black people in all avenues throughout their departments. In what was a very frank talk, I told them that racism has its costs—very large costs. For example, American companies spent $64 billion in 2007 alone to replace the talented professionals who had quit solely due to racial and sexual discrimination. That is expensive.

But was this just talk? Mellifluous ramblings that made everyone feel good for a few hours as they feasted on the idea of diversity? I took heart in the fact that I saw concrete action spring from these discussions. The clerk set up a deputy minister "champion" for visible minorities. The first champion was Morris Rosenberg, who was excellent and committed, and who moved the yardsticks. He was followed by George Da Pont, who told me of his serious efforts to provide more mentoring opportunities for Blacks at the executive level and, more importantly to me, that he was actively working to create more opportunities for horizontal movement to broaden experience and better support for networking. This is precisely what Blacks and other visible minorities had been lobbying for for years. So it *was* more than just mellifluous ramblings.

The Senate still seemed like a remote, distant entity that few people, even on Parliament Hill, knew much about. Similarly, few people understood the role of a deputy minister. Both groups are key players in developing public policy, but can often seem to one another like mysterious intellectuals in silk cocoons in distant ivory towers. Many senators had never spoken personally with a deputy minister, and many deputy ministers had never sat down with a senator. I wanted to change that. I started to host a series of small, private dinners with seven experienced senators and seven senior deputy ministers. I called them the "DM Dialogue Dinners." They were held three or four times a year at a private location; we broke bread and engaged in some fascinating debates about matters of difficult public policy that were in need of high-level legislative and bureaucratic analysis. These dinners connected the two solitudes of Canadian government. Some of the topics engaged the expertise of both senators and senior mandarins. Discussions included "How can the government work with non-governmental organizations (NGOs) to frame Canada's foreign policy?" and "What new public policies do we need to ensure Canada has safe and secure access to food?" or "How can entrepreneurial practices be applied to obtain higher social and financial returns from social development?" All of these were important, contemporary issues on which the legislative and bureaucratic branches could now work together.

This was a hopeful and wonderful sign for the future. It opened the door to allow both the legislative and senior bureaucratic sides to have input during the early stages of legislation. One deputy minister told me that these dinners provided "a safe space to discuss important public policy issues outside the formal setting of appearances before Senate committees."

Often, the meetings would have a special focus, and I would recruit seven experienced senators while my counterpart DM would do the same among the deputy ministers. This level of engagement helped make the dinner discussions successful. Soon, an invitation to participate at the DM table became a much sought-after item. And yet all the people I worked with at those tables were white. Where were all the Black people? What did that say about our government?

During all of these DM Dinners, there was no demonstration of anti-Black systemic racism, overt or otherwise. Why did white privilege not raise its head? What is the secret or the message we can derive from this and other such events? What were the similarities with the takeaways from the Linc Alexander gala dinner? Why was this a circumstance where I did not receive a constant reminder that I was different from most other Canadians? What seemed to make white privilege disappear?

The fact that deputy ministers were so engaged in these dinner discussions had helped open the door for me to personally engage the most senior bureaucrats in Canada to focus on anti-Black systemic racism in their departments, and this started to show some positive results. Our bond was an incredible asset when, as chair of the public relations and public sector committee of the BlackNorth Initiative (a project of the Canadian Council of Business Leaders Against Anti-Black Systemic Racism to encourage business leaders to acknowledge and address anti-Black systemic racism), I made an important connection. I personally introduced Ian Shugart, the clerk of the Privy Council, to Wes Hall, one of the most powerful Black business leaders in Canada, and a founder of the BlackNorth Initiative. At the outset, Ian expressed to Wes that he and I had been friends for "a hundred years," and in that forty-five minute tele-conference with the three of us that friendship shone through like magic. Suddenly—almost instantly—doors previously shut to Hall opened in an almost miraculous way. Personal relationships matter.

Another important factor is that all of this happened away from media and communications people, which gave us space to change attitudes and challenge stereotypes. This was all a very special use of my time as a senator.

❧

I was fortunate to be able to take the message of equality, tolerance, and diversity to a number of places around the world, and one of the most unique was Chiapas, Mexico. It is Mexico's most southerly region, bordering Guatemala. It is a beautiful, historic area of Mexico with tropical forests and many ancient Mayan archaeological sites, although I had no opportunity to explore them.

In October 2010, I was invited there as a keynote speaker at a parliamentary global conference designed to encourage the Indigenous peoples to organize, cooperate, and work with one another to find their way out of poverty.

Arriving at the Tuxtla Gutiérrez International Airport (also known as Ángel Albino Corzo Airport) in the city of Tuxtla Gutiérrez, Chiapas, I was met by a bodyguard and an interpreter, and we went to an armoured vehicle in the parking lot. My driver was armed. As we drove to my hotel, I wondered if I should be ducking my head to avoid the barrage of bullets that seemingly, at any moment, might be unleashed at our vehicle. How seriously should I take all this security?

The answer was: very seriously. Gangs had carried out violent crimes in the area. Looking out the car window, I saw some of the worst forms of poverty imaginable. The region had large Indigenous populations that were extremely poor, with extraordinarily high rates of illiteracy, and the highest rate of malnutrition in all of Mexico. The streets were not clean. There was garbage along the roadways, some of it stuck in the weeds and bushes.

The smell of poverty was everywhere. It was not a happy place. I went nowhere without my bodyguard and interpreter. I did not go outside the meeting hall, but went to the windows where I could see hundreds of Indigenous people, very poorly dressed, hands out, their eyes trying to catch mine, begging for money or food. Some looked as though they had not eaten for days. How could I help these people?

After registration at the hall, I was taken to my hotel and given instructions from the bodyguard on the program for the next day and on the steps I must take to stay safe, even in my hotel room. I reviewed my speaking notes, conscious of my privilege as I ate the sandwich that had been so readily provided to me. I took some deep breaths, just trying to take it all in.

The next morning, after I had made my presentation and was mingling with some of the other guests at the conference, I received a note from my Ottawa office with messages from our Department of Foreign Affairs. They said that David J. Thompson, the prime minister of Barbados, had just died of pancreatic cancer. He was just forty-eight, and his nation was plunged into mourning. The official state funeral was to take place in two days, November 3, at Kensington Oval stadium, and I was asked to be the official representative for the Government of Canada at the funeral. I had to leave the Chiapas conference early, flying to Mexico City, then Miami, and on to Barbados.

Barbados was hot, humid, and sticky. Thompson had a large following—supporters and friends who really loved him—and there were more than ten thousand people at the stadium, with more lining the road. Traffic everywhere was stalled. We just managed to get to the stadium in time to hear a moving series of tributes.

While I was in the country I expressed my condolences to the prime minister's family on behalf of Canada, and had brief bilateral meetings with a number of the representatives of Commonwealth countries who were present for the memorial. My mind flashed to the boyhood dream I'd had in Wolfville of growing up to be a diplomat. I felt I had achieved it, almost by accident.

What makes our Canadian way of life so unique and so different from that in authoritarian states like North Korea and Russia? It's our values—our intrinsic, inherent values of tolerance and diversity and our willingness to accept differences and not make fun of them. Since Confederation in 1867, we have gradually been casting off a lot of the old-country baggage of colonialism to form our own special Canadian identity. By the 1970s, that had led to a sense of pride in our multiculturalism, although that concept was certainly not universally understood or accepted throughout Canada. But that, and our bilingual policies, certainly defined Canada to the world. But there was still racism.

People around the world have asked me, what is Canada's secret? How can you get people who speak different languages, have different-coloured skin, wear different clothing, eat different foods, and have many other different habits, to live and work side by side in harmony? How is that possible?

The first part of the answer is because we are largely a nation of immigrants. The Indigenous peoples were here first, and the rest of us are all "from away." We learned to live with others from day one. We all contributed in our own humble ways to building a great nation of tolerance and understanding. As an African Nova Scotian, I am often asked where I come from. When I answer proudly that I am a third-generation Canadian, I get that quizzical stare: "Are you for real?"

Canada's neighbour to the south has a long-standing, ingrained culture of slavery, systemic racism, exclusion, and hatred toward people of African descent. Canada, sadly, has the same systemic problem, but probably not quite so ingrained. My grandparents on both sides are products of American slavery, and since that time the sting of racism has sadly hung over all of us for generations. For Black people, each step on our journey through life has involved carefully picking our way through a vast field of landmines, attempting to ensure we don't misstep or misspeak in order to avoid setting off another racial incident of outrageous proportions.

Growing up in small-town Nova Scotia, I read and heard about Old Black Joe, Aunt Jemima, and Al Jolson, "the king of the Blackface performers." I learned Blackface was a theatrical convention that had existed since the mid-nineteenth century and was widely in use well into the twentieth century. Blackface was a means to mock, ridicule, and demean people of African descent. In this racial stereotyping, Africans were depicted as lazy, ignorant, cowardly, and hyper-sexual. I even saw it a few years later on the face of Prime Minister Justin Trudeau. The leader of Canada's 37 million people of diverse backgrounds representing more than 250 ethnic groups put on a silly grin and Blackface makeup and saw nothing wrong with it at the time. This conduct was demeaning and hurtful to millions of Canadians. The fact that it was done by the prime minister of Canada repeatedly, without remorse or any apparent concern at the time, is as racist and offensive now as it was racist and offensive when it took place.

The prime minister's Blackface reinforced all the subtle distortions of hatred and mistrust people had of African culture, including a Black person's looks, language, deportment, and character. This is so sad. It cannot be the true face of Canada.

❖

As a senator I often travelled internationally, but some of my best trips were within Canada. That was the case in 2012, when work took me to Quebec City. Visiting Quebec City is like stepping into nineteenth-century Paris. The cobblestone streets and narrow alleyways in the walled Old Town highlight the old-world charm of the city. With its quaint little shops, restaurants, and bars, it is easy to pretend that you are stepping out with friends in Paris to enjoy a coffee or hot chocolate with a croissant. Of course, French is the sole official language in Quebec and about 80 percent of residents are francophone. The changing colours of the autumn leaves also present a stunning kaleidoscope throughout late September and early October each year.

The Historic District of Old Québec is a UNESCO World Heritage site that celebrates the city's European architecture and fortifications. Even the ancient houses with their bright-coloured shutters and doors take us back to Paris after the Napoleonic Wars. Throughout the walled city there are dozens of boutique cafés with all the Parisian classics like baguettes, pain au chocolat, macarons, mille feuille, eclairs, and lots of fruits and wine. There is always an abundance of quaint bistros serving the classic steak frites, and you could spend an entire afternoon visiting Quebec City's countless galleries filled with beautiful pieces from local artists.

It was the perfect place to host the Inter-Parliamentary Union (IPU), a global group of parliaments formed in 1889 and dedicated to promoting peace and cooperation among democracies. We gathered in October 2012, bringing parliamentarians representing 129 countries from around the globe to savour the romance and charm of Quebec City.

There were a total of 1,256 delegates, 624 of whom were members of national parliaments. After working my way through the chairmanships of many committees, groups, and assemblies, I was finally able to persuade the largest assembly of parliaments on the globe—all 162 of them—and 10 regional parliamentary assemblies, to come to Canada instead of Geneva for the fall meeting. This was an enormous coup for Canada. This would be the largest parliamentary assembly ever held in Canada. I had spent dozens

Senator Donald Oliver helped organize the 127th Assembly of the Inter-Parliamentary Union in Quebec. It was the largest parliamentary conference ever held in Canada, and it's clear from Oliver's smile that he was pleased to take part, given that the theme of the conference—Citizenship, Identity, and Linguistic and Cultural Diversity in a Globalized World—was an ideal match for his own public policy interests. (Courtesy the Senate of Canada)

of hours over many months, and indeed years, to make this a reality. We met for five days, not the usual three. The theme was "Citizenship, Identity, and Linguistic and Cultural Diversity in a Globalized World." I could not have been more pleased and excited by the theme. But the real intrigue behind the scenes of the event was so intense and difficult that several spy thrillers could have come out of it.

For example, there is a clear rule of the governing council of the IPU that says, "IPU assemblies can only be held if all IPU members and observers are invited and if their representatives are certain to be granted visas required for participation." As a sovereign state, Canada has the right to determine to whom it will and will not grant visas. There were states like Syria, Iran, and Zimbabwe, with whom Canada had foreign policy issues. Nevertheless, these countries were members in good standing with the IPU and were demanding visas in accordance with established rules. If this blew up and the assembly was cancelled, Canada would be looked down upon by dozens and dozens of countries around the globe for breaching an international agreement. I was under enormous pressure to somehow, as assembly chair, intervene with Canadian visa officials to expedite the granting of all necessary visas.

I was on the phone several times every hour with the Prime Minister's Office, the Privy Council office, the protocol office, the chief administrative officers of the IPU, and, for example, the representatives of the speaker from Zimbabwe who had to make travel reservations to fly to Quebec City from Harare. The pressure continued to mount. No one wanted to give an inch. I had serious visions of the entire assembly collapsing and a volley of lawsuits being launched to recover the costs of cancelled flights and hotels. Finally there was a massive compromise—everyone gave something somehow—and the show went on. What a relief. Our minister of foreign affairs gave a welcoming opening address that touched on the visa issues, but the conference went on to be an overwhelming success.

Throughout most of my career in the Senate, I was a very active member of the IPU, which had observer status at the United Nations. I actually gave a major speech on the economic importance of remittances—the act of sending money back to one's home country—at an IPU inquiry held at the UN in New York. Just as it did with the United Nations, the IPU actually had a direct relationship with a number of these Geneva-based international organizations. One of them was with the World Trade Organization. Earlier in 2012 I had chaired the annual Parliamentary Conference on the World Trade Organization in Geneva, co-organized by the IPU and the European Union. The annual gathering allows parliamentarians to engage in trade issues, and our presence in the WTO ensures more legitimacy and democracy. This meeting brought together legislators from more than seventy different countries including China, Germany, France, India, and Brazil.

Even before the conference began, a great deal of research had been undertaken to determine if the WTO, the only global international organization dealing with the rules of trade between nations, should have a parliamentary or legislative dimension. In what way could a world body of parliaments be of help to the functioning of the WTO? The obvious response is that it would be the ideal vehicle for providing and ensuring parliamentary oversight.

But it is best explained by Pascal Lamy, director-general of the WTO, who said at our conference:

> *The link between the house of parliament (IPU), and the house of trade (WTO), is extremely important to the WTO for one simple reason, which is that we believe we are accountable to parliamentarians….We believe that this accountability and your own engagement and involvement in our trade issues are a good way to strengthen the multilateral trading system and provide legitimacy for what we do.*

The conference reconfirmed the significant role legislators must play in the formulation of integrated and coherent national trade, industry, labour market, and social policies. Indeed, it provided strong political leadership and guidance on trade and economic policy. One of the things I recall distinctly about chairing the 2012 conference was that there was vigorous debate about trade as a tool of economic growth, job creation, and poverty alleviation. We also looked at the challenge for trade in the twenty-first century, appealing to the WTO to leverage trade to create good jobs now for a future where financial instability will likely persist.

I was successful in achieving a resolution for an "open, non-discriminatory, and fair multilateral trading system that can effectively contribute to economic growth, sustainable development, and employment generation." All of that, with the assistance back home of parliamentarians in their own legislative bodies, made the case for those three main outcomes: economic growth, sustainable development, and employment generation. Now that's an achievement of global proportions from a "backbench nobody"!

Pascal Lamy is a French intellectual with whom I had the honour to work on a few occasions. He was a powerful and busy man, and I really enjoyed being with him. It was not conceivable to simply sit down and have a casual conversation with him over coffee at a bar. He was, in a sense, like a rock star. When he came into the room, the sea of people opened up like the parting of the Red Sea. Everyone wanted to talk to him. Most delegates had trade questions for him from their home parliaments or governments, so you can imagine that he had to be carefully escorted from one room to the next with some security and protection. Conversations were on a strictly "as needed" basis.

In some of his contemporary writings, and at large public assemblies, he would often speak of the need for a "new world order," and he would describe what our multilateral organizations should look like going forward. As the world changes, he noted, so must our largest global institutions adjust and change. I was honoured to have a few good discussions with him about a parliamentary dimension to the WTO, and, in fact, I was asked to participate in making a video on the very subject, which I did, and it ran for years on the WTO website. Pascal was a visionary and a thinker. He felt passionately that all the world's largest organizations had to learn to adapt as the world constantly changed through globalization, financial crises, or the emergence of things like the European Union.

I found his vision and theories of the new world order challenging and fascinating. He was also very charismatic. He spoke with a strong French accent over his very large brown tinted glasses, pronouncing each word and phrase slowly, distinctly, and with deep feeling. When he spoke to a group, you could almost hear a pin drop because most in attendance knew he would have something thoughtful to say.

His position was that globalization had changed and we needed a new world order to accommodate the social, economic, and political needs of the day. The G20 had replaced the G8 and it provided some leadership and direction. The WTO took decisions by consensus, but that was part of its weakness because it might not provide the sense of legitimacy the world needed. In addition to the G20, member-driven international organizations would have to become more active, and adding a political dimension by a restructuring of the 192-member UN might create a forum for accountability. But even that structure needed a set of new core values similar to German chancellor Angela Merkel's "charter of sustainable economic activity."

The above theory needs one more dimension—the IPU, our parliaments, as the voices of the people. The governance system the world seeks today will be ineffective unless citizens of the world have a forum or an avenue for shaping tomorrow's world. That's the background against which I spoke and debated in the video for the WTO website. That whole experience had a major impact on my thinking and it strengthened my own understanding of the world—and, I hope, made me a better politician. To be the one parliamentarian on the globe chosen to champion a liaison with the world's parliaments and the World Trade Organization was one of the great achievements of my life.

Those are but a few of the rewarding work assignments I had the privilege to take on during my twenty-three-year political career.

As the insightful Robert Stanfield once said about his own political career, they "gave a depth and meaning to my life that I had no right to expect." They gave me a chance to live a life that was multifaceted, active, and imbued with vigour. The IPU also provided me with a global platform for promoting the value of diversity and the importance of tolerance.

After all that, I could see retirement on the horizon—but I did not see the surprising obstacles that were about to spring up.

Chapter Twelve

RETIREMENT

IN 2013, AS I APPROACHED MY SEVENTY-FIFTH BIRTHDAY—
the mandatory age for retirement from the Senate—I had tentative
plans to work on a number of business projects in Africa and, if
you can imagine it, I was going to be a partner in building a huge,
state-of-the-art sugar refinery in Uganda. I also had some prelimi-
nary ideas for financial proposals with Sunir Chandaria, a Canadian
businessman whose family was well known in Africa. But in the
summer of that year, my good friend, brilliant serial entrepreneur
Wade Dawe of Halifax, asked me to accompany him on a business
trip to Gabon in central Africa. That was a huge honour.

Wade had investments in different parts of Africa. Whenever
he enters a new space or a new situation and he hears new ideas and
sees new things, he almost instantly visualizes a business opportunity—a way of building things from scratch to make money for his
shareholders and himself. He sees opportunities most of us miss.
Wade is chairman of Fortune Bay, a gold exploration and development company, and he built and sold Brigus Gold to Primero Mining
in 2014 for $351 million. He has completed many deals amounting to

more than a billion dollars, and along the way has created a number of successful companies that I am happy to have bought shares in on the open market.

Today the world is transitioning into clean technologies, and that is a direction in which Wade's major investment vehicle and merchant bank, Torrent Capital, is looking. During our trip to Africa, a number of unexpected hurdles tested Wade's genius and his strong moral values. He is principled and has extremely high ethical standards for all with whom he is associated. I learned a lot from him about how personal ethical standards must be applied in large global investment deals.

Gabon is a small democratic republic with a bicameral (two-chambered) legislature. It has a population of over 2.2 million, and covers a land area of 257,000 square kilometres. The head of state is President Ali Bongo Ondimba. Its economy is driven principally by oil, timber, and manganese. I was to arrange meetings in Libreville, the capital, with all the leading government ministers and ministries, which I did. Gabon's Speaker, Sophie Moulengui-Mouele Ngouamassana, invited me to drop by her office and pay respects while in Libreville. She was one of the most powerful and well-connected women in the country. Wade already had some considerable mining investment assets and land leases in Gabon, but now, before investing further capital, was the time to talk with government officials about their public policy initiatives in mining and trade for the short term and long term.

The official language of Gabon is French, so I made use of my limited French language skills. We met one-on-one with the ministers of mines, industry, finance, trade, and investment and I had arranged private dinners and lunches with other key investment figures, both in and out of government. In addition, we spent time with Wade's own employees there to receive up-to-date reports and samples of the excavation. The meetings and dinners all went exceptionally well, and the government and non-government officials we met were all deeply impressed by Wade, and encouraged him, in the strongest of terms, to continue to invest in Gabon.

But during the course of our meetings with the local employees, some matters came up that were of deep ethical concern to Wade and me. We discussed them, and after interviews with a number of people there was no question about the resolution that was required to the problem. I was impressed with Wade's detailed analysis of the complicated issues at hand and why they had to be dealt with immediately. Good ethics always stood above profits and positive return on investment. All the necessary decisions were taken with staff and we left for Canada and there were no more investments in Gabon. Wade had demonstrated to me some of the highest principles of good corporate governance. He was and remains a great mentor and good personal friend.

❖

When I prepared to retire from the Senate on November 16, 2013, I wrote and circulated a final newsletter highlighting some of the key work I'd done during my twenty-three years in that chamber. "Little did I know when I was growing up in Wolfville, Nova Scotia, in the 1940s and 1950s that one day this little Black kid from a poor family would one day become a senator," I wrote. "Never in my wildest dreams!" I served Canadians for 8,472 days in the Senate. I rose in the chamber 279 times to call the honourable senators' attention to important happenings or events, usually related to matters of inclusion, tolerance, and diversity.

I had given a total of 1,279 Senate speeches. It had been my privilege to be the chairman of five standing committees of the Senate, and co-chair of a special joint committee of the House of Commons and the Senate on a Code of Conduct. After that report (called by some the Oliver–Milligan report) hit the internet, co-author Peter Milligan and I were invited to Warsaw, Poland, to address the academic and senior bureaucratic communities in panel discussions, debates, and lectures about our report. We had a wonderful, frank exchange of ideas. The parliamentarians in Poland liked it so much that our code was subsequently adopted into law as the ethical code of conduct for parliamentarians in Poland. Back home, I had the opportunity to tell Prime Minister Jean Chrétien that Poland had adopted our code before the Canadian Parliament had adopted it. "It will happen," he assured me, "it will happen soon."

In my maiden speech in the Senate, I made it clear who I was and where I came from. Among many other things, I said that through my appointment to the Senate, I believed I could "represent Black Nova Scotians, and visible minorities, throughout the country. As a member of both communities, I understand the need to combat racism whenever it appears, and to provide equal opportunities to all, regardless of the colour of your skin."

Even though I lived virtually all my life with a constant reminder that I was different from most Canadians, and even though I knew that somehow I must prove that I was worthy to participate in and enjoy all the fruits that have been bestowed on the white majority because of their privilege, I managed to survive. Moreover I was able to make a difference by openly promoting tolerance, understanding, and diversity, which in their own ways help to break down the stigma of systemic anti-Black racism. As a human-rights activist, I was able to challenge the intellectual mindset of certain whites by encouraging them to explore some uncomfortable truths. Being appointed a senator was one of the key levers that gave me the power to be able to make a difference, particularly in making the business case for diversity around the globe.

It was the end of an era. In 2013, after twenty-three of the best years of my life, I retired from the Senate of Canada. I returned my keys to the Senate office, along with all the passes, codes, credit cards, computers, and cellphones. I retained my personal cellphone and an iPad.

The lease was up on our Ottawa apartment, leaving Linda and me with no place to sleep. I booked a nice room at the Château Laurier. Our plan was to take a leisurely drive home to Nova Scotia in the following day or two. We hired movers to handle the big things, but somehow enough stuff was left over to stuff the car to the brim. We were like young kids just starting out in our car filled with dishes, paintings, books, and clothes, all jumbled up in the jungle of the back seat and trunk. We were in no rush to get back home.

That first evening, Linda and I sat in the lounge at the Château Laurier. I noticed Linda was frowning at me. What had I done wrong? I wondered. Then I noticed my hand had crept across the table to my phone and picked it up. The habit was so ingrained, I hadn't even noticed I was doing it—and during my first evening of retirement, on a date with my wife. Linda reached for my Blackberry. I was so surprised I just handed it to her without question.

"We're retired," she said, looking a little anxious. "Let's forget about people sending emails. Let's have a champagne toast to celebrate our freedom. I'm putting my Blackberry away as well."

We had both retired that day. We were drinking champagne, her favourite drink, to celebrate. We smiled at each other. She turned my phone off. Later, hers buzzed in her pocket. She ignored it. It was a night just for us. Over dinner, we dreamed up a bucket list for our new life. Her phone buzzed again. She ignored it. At the sleepy end of the day, we retired to our room. She slipped her phone out of her pocket and checked to see what all the fuss had been about. It had buzzed all evening.

"Oh my!" she exclaimed. "There is a message from the Prime Minister's Office. They've been trying to reach you."

She played the message. The caller apologized for bothering Linda, but "the senator appeared to have his BlackBerry turned off. It is very important that the senator call the PMO immediately."

So much for the tranquility of retirement! Linda looked at her missed calls and found she had been bombarded by the PMO all evening as people tried to find me. I turned on my phone and called the staffer back right away, wondering what on Earth could cause Prime Minister Stephen Harper to need a retired farmer so urgently in the late evening. "The prime minister is inviting you to join him on the plane to Nelson Mandela's memorial service in South Africa. We leave tomorrow," the staffer said.

I was wide awake, sitting bolt upright with my heart hammering away. Oh my God! What an honour! It was an incredible surprise. I had mourned with the rest of the world when Mandela had died, but it had never crossed my mind that I would be permitted to pay tribute in person to such an influential leader. We all could learn so much from his teachings and from the way he conducted himself, particularly in difficult situations. He embraced his enemies and promoted forgiveness and racial reconciliation. He showed no signs of bitterness or hatred.

So much for not checking my BlackBerry over dinner. I nearly missed out on a once-in-a-lifetime trip. It then occurred to me that I might still have missed out, but the staffer told me it was not too late—so long as I was on the plane in Ottawa at "wheels up" at 5:00 P.M. the next day. I had to fly to Halifax, drive to my home some two hours away, pack the clothes I needed for a formal funeral, drive back to the airport, return the rented car, fly back to Ottawa, and find my way to the secure area to get the plane to South Africa.

I made it, but only with the incredible assistance of Scott McCord, my long-time friend and excellent travel agent from Ottawa, who worked late into the evening to arrange all the flights and other particulars for this undertaking. I could not have made it without him.

Prime Minister Harper invited me to join him in the front section of the plane. We were both Conservatives and had worked well together over our shared years in government. He often sought me out for one-on-one meetings about public policy, diversity in the workplace, and other issues. The first time we'd had such a meeting, we had scheduled thirty minutes but ended up talking for an hour. He truly understood the blight of systemic anti-Black racism and the evils of unchained hatred. He had already arranged for my personal meeting with President Obama, and now he'd ensured I would be among the small group of Canadians to observe President Mandela's memorial.

I took my comfortable seat and looked around me in wonder. Former governor general Michaëlle Jean sat in front of me. Former prime minister Kim Campbell sat beside me. Former prime minister Jean Chrétien sat in front of her. Across the aisle, I saw former prime minister Brian Mulroney and former governor general Adrienne Clarkson. I was so overwhelmed by the change in my situation that I could hardly speak. But given that it was a nineteen-hour flight, I soon relaxed and enjoyed the chance to socialize with such a decorated group of people. We represented different political parties, but we were all going to South Africa as Canadians.

Once the fasten-seatbelt light turned off, people started swapping seats to chat with one another. Brian Mulroney, Kim Campbell, and Jean Chrétien kept the rest of us on the edges of our seats as they told stories about things only prime ministers would encounter. Adrienne Clarkson and Brian Mulroney both love to sing and knew all the oldies, and they created some great music to pass the time.

We finally arrived in Johannesburg and were escorted to our hotel rooms to prepare for what would certainly be an exciting next day. The memorial service was held at FNB Stadium in Soweto, which seats 95,000 people, but it was not filled. The weather did not cooperate at all. Heavy rain made the job of protocol and security officers even more difficult. Everything was backed up. Nothing was happening on time. The South African protocol office was overwhelmed with logistical problems, including a power failure that held up more than 30,000 people. It was sometimes pouring rain, both outside and inside parts of the stadium. A kaleidoscope of multi-coloured, multi-designed umbrellas created a sort of rainbow throughout the stadium in that rainbow nation.

In attendance was a dazzling array of royalty, statesmen, business elites, and, yes, celebrities like Bono, the lead singer of U2. People from a hundred nations had gathered to honour Mandela and all that South Africa had achieved with him. On the morning of the memorial, our Canadian group was transported to the waiting area for the stadium. Our credentials were checked, and countries were arranged and lined up in the order in which they would be entering the stadium to sit in their pre-selected seats.

I was standing at the side of the room, listening and observing in awe when a nervous and obviously new protocol officer suddenly spoke up. He was surrounded by a few thousand dignitaries and, with sweat dripping from his brow as he grasped a handful of paper, he explained in a loud voice that he wanted guests to line up in order of seniority after he called their names. "We will start with presidents and prime ministers," he said. A voice interrupted from the back: "What about kings and queens? Where do they stand?" That would, I presume, include Prince Charles, who was there. I noticed the people standing by the door quietly backing up to clear a path for the royals. I gave a grateful grin, delighted that I didn't have those problems.

There were a lot of other famous people from around the world present to pay their respects to such a pillar of a man who had changed the world. Richard Branson was in attendance. Oprah Winfrey was also there. She has made such a powerful impression on the world as someone who believes that Black lives matter—and has since long before the movement began. I would have loved to meet her.

Our Canadian group then was moved to another, much smaller, waiting room with a smaller group. Bono sauntered over, shook hands and chatted with Jean Chrétien and many others. People were coming and going from all directions, shaking hands, hugging one another, taking selfies, and throwing kisses if they could not get close enough. There was a real buzz in the room.

The memorial was, as an African person in the stadium put it, "a time of sadness celebrated by song and dance." Before the memorial started, bands and singers on the main stage performed a number of songs and dances that had the name Mandela (Madiba) in them, songs from the era of the apartheid struggle to modern, liberated South Africa. "Mandela," with its three vowels, is a musical sound and it bounced to the rhythms of many songs. As the heavy rain continued to fall on the stadium, the memorial fell behind schedule. A part of me reflected that I had expected on this day to be meandering along the back roads of New Brunswick and Nova Scotia, making my way to the solitude of the farm with Linda. Yet here I was in Africa, among people from all over the world.

When I got to my seat, I was awestruck by the enormity of the stadium and the noise from many different bands and singers, both inside and outside the stadium. All the songs were sung with incredibly engaging harmonies and counterpoint to very complex African rhythms that made everyone want to sway their bodies to the rhythm. Horns were blowing, flags were waving, people were sharing in this celebration of the life of Mandela, Mandela, Madiba, Madiba.

There was a loud hum from thousands of people all talking at once. On top of that, drums were beating, people were singing songs and chants; indeed, many different bands played during this glorious celebration. The memorial service finally started with all the formality one would expect, but the massive crowd in the stadium was hard to control. Everyone wanted to talk, and the bands simply did not want to stop playing. The emcee called for order over and over and begged the bands to stop the music. It was a losing battle.

The event was televised, recorded, and live-streamed; we could see what was happening on big screens near us and could hear the commentators pointing out who was who. When President Barack Obama went to the stage to give his powerful speech, he received the largest ovation of the day. Everyone loved him—the most powerful man in the world. He spoke about Mandela bringing people together. Later, the cameras caught him coming together with Danish Prime Minister Helle Thorning-Schmidt and British Prime Minister David Cameron for a selfie. The smiles and laughter between Barack and Helle were also caught on-camera by the media and nearly caused a minor international incident because their conduct was considered a bit too familiar.

I thought back to my first trip to South Africa in 1994, when Mandela had first been elected president of the free republic. The United Nations had sent me as an observer to those elections. When the voting started in my area, every day I could see people, elderly people, thousands of people, colourfully dressed and in lines longer than the eye could see, who had walked for miles, some in bare feet, anxious to mark their first ballot. I was dressed in my blue UN vest and matching hat and I was authorized to enter polling stations and voting booths to assist voters as needed.

One elderly gentleman, smartly dressed, crouched over and supported by a homemade cane, had ventured into a voting booth, but did not exit. "Do you need any help, sir?" I finally asked.

No response. I asked again. Finally, he murmured softly, "Mandela, Mandela." His voice was calm with love and affection. "Mandela," he repeated, pointing to the complex voting document. I showed him where Mandela was on the ballot and he made his mark.

It was a deeply moving experience for me. I can still hear that gentleman humbly uttering, "Mandela, Mandela." It went to the heart of my African experience.

Chapter Thirteen

A LIFE-
CHANGING
DIAGNOSIS

AFTER RETIRING TO MY FARM, WHICH I LOVED SO DEARLY, IN rural Nova Scotia, I continued to give speeches on the business case for diversity. I was invited in 2015 to give a lecture to a combined group of business students from the Rotman School of Management and the Munk School of Global Affairs and Public Policy, both in Toronto. I was excited to challenge these bright young minds with the data to prove that a diverse workplace adds value to a corporation's bottom line, and that a diverse board can help an organization get away from groupthink. I wanted to prove to them that board and executive diversity would improve the bottom line.

I arrived at the school early to check out the general set-up of the room, the sound equipment, and the computer for slides. It was in a new, modern building. There was a lot of shiny marble and glass. The student who was assigned to meet me at the entrance wanted to introduce me to the school's president. When the president learned that I had not been there before, he kindly offered to give me a quick tour.

He began walking fairly quickly up a series of steps while pointing out where various classes were held and which benefactors funded which wings and rooms, when suddenly it happened. My heart pounded. I struggled to breathe. He continued up the steps, not noticing my distress. I stopped and gasped. Finally, he realized I'd stopped and turned to ask if I was okay. I said I was, but this had never happened to me before. I felt embarrassed. I asked the president if we could use an elevator.

I made it to the classroom and delivered a forty-five-minute lecture before taking questions. I barely made it through the lecture and the question period. I was tired, felt weak, had difficulty breathing, and was frankly not thinking clearly. I stayed in a hotel overnight and the next day I flew to Halifax and then drove home.

Linda immediately noticed I was struggling to climb the thirteen steps from the main floor to the second floor of our house. At her urging, I called my family doctor's office. He called me back and asked a few questions.

"I do not like what I'm hearing," he told me. "Where is the nearest hospital? Go there now. I'll phone the hospital and tell them you're coming."

I arrived at the South Shore Regional Hospital in Bridgewater, NS, weak and very tired. Linda helped me through the standard emergency protocols and I was admitted almost immediately to Emergency. They assessed my vital signs, gave me an IV, and put me in a bed. They told me I was in congestive heart failure, with an ejection fraction of 14 percent (a normal ejection fraction is between 55 and 70 percent). My heart was basically non-functional. My doctor told me they suspected that I had a rare, incurable heart disease, and that I had six months to live. "Where do you want to die?" the doctor asked.

I didn't want to die. I had just retired after working for fifty-one years. Linda had retired on the same day I did. We had a bucket list—kicking the bucket wasn't on it. I'd been looking forward to spending my golden years helping the Black community, travelling, spending time with family, doing charitable work, taking cruises, gardening, and playing golf.

Instead, I was in the hospital. They drained fifteen pounds of fluid from my body, some of which had made it to my lungs. They used medications to stabilize my heart, which was beating in a rapid, irregular, and highly worrying rhythm. They told me the irregular rhythm could cause a blood clot that could trigger a damaging stroke. My ankles and feet swelled up.

For the next six days and five nights I stayed in the hospital, hardly moving amid a flurry of medical treatments. I was then sent to the heart clinic in Halifax, where cardiologists took several biopsies of my heart and sent them to the Mayo Clinic in Rochester, Minnesota. The Mayo had a mass spectrometer, which Nova Scotia did not have, and which was used to analyze my biopsied heart tissues.

Once the diagnosis was confirmed I met with a specialist in Halifax. The doctor, reading from the Mayo Clinic report, told me I had a rare disease called cardiac Amyloidosis. A faulty gene in the liver caused it. No one knew how to cure it. And the "good news" was that I didn't need to take a bone biopsy or think about chemotherapy. This doctor strongly suggested it was time for me to get my affairs in order—update my will; plan my funeral. That hit me like a ton of bricks. I went numb. Six months to live? Death was suddenly on the horizon.

"Do you know what palliative care is?" she asked me.

I turned my head, ignoring the question. She looked at me closely and in a raised voice repeated the question. "They can make the last two months of your life comfortable," she added.

I told her I knew what palliative care meant. She said I should phone them that day and meet with them as soon as I could. I agreed. Linda, always at my side, disagreed. "We don't have to make that decision now," she said.

I was stunned into silence. Linda, holding the Mayo Clinic report, looked at the doctor.

"If it were you, what would you do?" she asked.

"There is no hospital, clinic, or doctor in Canada with the expertise to treat this rare disease. I would get a referral to the Mayo Clinic," the doctor answered.

"Can you help us with the paperwork?" Linda asked.

The doctor agreed to write a letter and she had it ready the next day. Suddenly, all my hopes were pinned on the Mayo Clinic.

❖

It's a long way from the farm to the Mayo Clinic. The simplest route I could find went farm-to-Halifax-to-Toronto-to-Minneapolis-to-Rochester. It's a tiring trip that takes the best part of a day. I was now using a cane, a walker, and sometimes a wheelchair, because I was weak, light-headed, could not walk without getting seriously out of breath, and certainly could not walk up the steep ramps from where the airplanes docked. I was not able to travel by myself, so I needed Linda, my caregiver, for support, which meant two airline tickets, two meals, and so on.

When I arrived at the world-famous Mayo Clinic, it struck me as some kind of wonderland. The hospital was like a self-contained town, with its own huge laundry and transportation systems. Rochester, in the heart of Minnesota, is not a big place, and a lot of the architecture looks fairly modern, but the Mayo Clinic itself is huge. There is a main complex of high-rise buildings in the centre of town, and other Mayo Clinic offices, hospitals, and research centres all over town. Overhead and underground passageways connected several of the large downtown buildings where I most frequently found myself.

Virtually all medical procedures and practice were online and computerized. All my personal health records were accessible online and I had my own patient's portal. Thousands of physicians, medical specialists, and scientists work for this seamless but highly complex organization. Some days, I had five appointments at five different places, but there was never a wait or a delay.

Dr. Martha Grogan, a world-renowned specialist in cardiac Amyloidosis, met with us for an hour and a half. I was given a lot of advice on what must be done next, given my current weakened condition with serious muscle-wasting. After all my appointments, I made the long trip back to the farm. That Sunday morning, our phone rang. It was Dr. Grogan, who was with her husband at their cottage in Wisconsin, and she said she had been thinking about my case and wanted to give me some additional advice. She recommended I take certain steps immediately and then return to Mayo in Rochester. A Sunday morning, off-duty call from a leading world expert from her summer cottage—that is one of the reasons the clinic has such a reputation for excellence.

There were no miracle drugs or known treatments that could cure me. Normally medical professionals would simply try to keep a patient like me comfortable. But Dr. Grogan was aware of a clinical trial for a new drug that was thought to be able to silence the bad gene in my liver. It was a gene called V122l that was causing all the problems. After several days of tests (and prayers, on my part) I was admitted to the clinical trial. It was a double-blind trial, which meant that I did not know whether I was being given the placebo or the actual drug. I had my fingers crossed that it was the drug. I took part in the study for more than a year, which involved frequent trips to Rochester from Halifax, but the good news was that I sensed, and my wife sensed, that I was starting to feel a bit better. I must have been getting the real drug, not the placebo, and it must have been working to silence the offending gene.

I returned to the Mayo Clinic for more tests and had just finished an MRI when a technician told me Dr. Grogan was waiting in the next room to speak to me right away. She was a long way from her office, and I wondered what could prompt such a personal encounter. She broke the bad news: the company that made the drug had terminated the trial and I would no longer be able to get it.

I was floored. I felt certain the drug was doing good things for me. I wrote to the CEO of the pharmaceutical company to give him my layman's view. After the trial was cancelled, I found out that I had, in fact, been on the drug and not on the placebo.

In the meantime, I had developed quite severe neuropathy, and there was another new drug that was ready for clinical trial. After months of trying, Dr. Grogan managed to get me enrolled. For this trial, instead of me taking an expensive trip to the Mayo Clinic every three weeks, a registered nurse comes to my house, where I sit on my comfortable chair and drink tea while she does the treatments.

❖

Amid all that turmoil, I received two great honours in 2020—bright lights in my twilight years: the Order of Canada and the Order of Nova Scotia. The Order of Canada is one of our country's highest civilian honours. It recognizes outstanding achievement, dedication to the community, and service to the nation. It is the cornerstone of the Canadian honours system. The brief citation read, "Donald H. Oliver, Halifax and Ottawa. For his untiring efforts as a senator, educator, and civic-minded community member who promotes inclusion and diversity in Canada." It is humbling to read this citation even now.

The Order of Nova Scotia is the highest honour given by the province. It recognizes Nova Scotians for their outstanding achievements and contributions. Members have distinguished themselves in many fields of endeavour and have brought honour and prestige to themselves and to Nova Scotia. The award cited my promotion of inclusion, tolerance, fairness, and diversity as a key achievement of my life's work. That was also clearly stated in a personal letter sent to me from Dr. Peter Ricketts, president and vice-chancellor of Acadia University, in which he wrote, "It is also a testament to your lifelong contribution to the community for more than 50 years as a human-rights advocate and trailblazer, breaking down barriers of racism and intolerance and promoting inclusion and diversity here at home and around the world."

Darlene Norman, the mayor of the Region of Queens Municipality, where I live, said in a very kind congratulatory letter, "Your renowned aunt, Portia White, is quoted to have said, 'First you dream and then you lace up your boots.' You have indeed laced up your boots and your dreams have led you to be a man of great vision."

Both awards assured me I had enjoyed a life well lived.

But it was an award not in my name that was one of the really powerful moments for me. I had met Nova Scotia businessperson Ron Joyce years ago, in the 1960s when I was starting out in law. At that time, I wanted to invest in a fast-food restaurant to develop my business interests so I could put more money toward Black education. I wanted to create more scholarships and bursaries for Black students, and other prizes to reward scholars of African descent. The Senator Donald Oliver Bursary for students of African descent, at Dalhousie University, had been generously created by my brother-in-law Hugh Maccagno. Having matched his initial founding donation,

I wanted to add to that fund, perhaps through a successful investment in a Tim Hortons franchise.

Back then, Ron seemed to be doing well with his Tim Hortons start-up, selling coffee and donuts. It seemed to be growing quickly, so perhaps this was the opportunity for me. I did my due diligence and decided to throw an oar in the water and submit an application for a store licence in Nova Scotia. Two weeks later, I received a phone call at home from a number in Hamilton, Ontario. It was Ron, who spoke with an affable but gruff business-sounding voice.

"I've got your application in front of me," he said. "You qualify financially, but there was one matter I decided I wanted to phone you about. In your form you state you will build it and later have a business manager run it for you. That is not our business model; franchises must be owner-operated." I told him I had other businesses that were run for me by managers and that they were working out well.

I knew that because I had a busy law practice I didn't have the time it would take to run a franchise, so we wrapped up the call. But we stayed in touch over the years and met for business discussions, often at the same dinner table, at business meetings in Toronto. When we met, I talked about the difficulties Black youth faced in trying to get an education. Ron listened with interest.

In 2000, he built an exceptional, jaw-droppingly beautiful golf resort known as Fox Harb'r in Nova Scotia. I did some business entertaining there, and when he was around, he was always one of my guests. He was an exceptional businessman and it was not long before Tim Hortons overtook McDonald's, gaining the largest market share in the fast food industry in Canada. By the time he'd sold Tim Hortons he had substantially increased his philanthropic and charitable giving. One day while meeting at Fox Harb'r, Ron told me he wanted to create something at Acadia University, and to do it in my name.

I was deeply touched and honoured, but I had another idea. Since the White and Oliver families had devoted more than a century to working for and promoting Acadia University, and had advanced education as part of their DNA, I suggested he name the award for my parents. Soon enough, a million-dollar endowment launched the annual Clifford and Helena Oliver Bursaries for students of African descent, worth $5,000 per year for a four-year total of $20,000 per student. It was an exceptionally kind gift.

Chapter 14

THE LEGACY OF GEORGE FLOYD

THE WORLD GOT A HORRIFYING DEMONSTRATION OF ANTI-Black racism on May 21, 2020, when George Perry Floyd Jr., an African American, was brutally murdered without cause. The world watched in real time as a white police officer, Derek Chauvin, put his knee on Floyd's neck and kept pressing. With his face on the ground and his hands and legs restrained, Floyd could be heard crying out and pleading for help. "I can't breathe," he gasped as the police officer pressed harder on his neck and held it for more than nine minutes. Suddenly Floyd was no longer breathing. The forty-six-year-old truck driver and security guard from Minneapolis, Minnesota, was dead.

This spectacle was watched live by millions around the world, but no one came to offer any help. It was classic white against Black. It was the epitome of anti-Black systemic racism. Was this Black man not worthy of help? The world got an unfiltered look at white privilege.

People of African descent were regarded as separate beings within a society normalized as white. They looked different with their Black skin, so they could be treated differently.

Our system needs reform. This was not simply a case of a white police officer killing a Black man in broad daylight without motive or excuse. This calls into play the need for an in-depth analysis of the political, economic, and social infrastructure that would permit this to happen. Millions of people and global organizations responded to this outrage. Amnesty International delivered a letter with one million signatures from around the world to the US attorney general, demanding justice for George Floyd. The tragedy strengthened the Black Lives Matter movement and human rights and civil liberties organizations around the globe had to respond.

And not only political organizations responded. The Royal Bank of Canada, one of the largest companies in Canada with more than eighty thousand employees and assets exceeding $1.43 trillion, also felt it was necessary to learn and react accordingly. The bank had a committee it called the Global Diversity Leadership Council, which the bank's chief executive officer chaired and which had a number of the bank's senior Black employees as members. The CEO, Dave McKay, a white man, started having conversations with some Black employees on the Council. He called on them to speak out about some of their daily experiences as Black men and women. Their horrendous stories of encountering racism while they were shopping, eating in restaurants, taking their kids to school, and attending sports activities began rolling out, and the senior white bankers present had their eyes opened. McKay, in shock, admitted, "We never listened." He agreed they had to do something about it.

"When you have that type of systemic racism you can't say your community is healthy," he said. "We were never sensitized to how serious the issue was." That floored me. Never sensitized! So that was the beginning in corporate Canada of exploring some uncomfortable truths about white privilege and systemic anti-Black racism. The private sector, represented by the largest corporations, and the public sector, represented by the bureaucracies in federal, provincial, municipal, and territorial governments, all had to be *taught* the uncomfortable truths about white privilege.

I wrote about it in a widely read column for the *Globe and Mail*. So did my friend, the powerful Bay Street Black businessman Wes Hall. He said it was time for Black leadership in Canada to stand up and be counted and to work hand-in-hand with our corporate and bureaucratic giants to bring about meaningful change. He founded a not-for-profit called the BlackNorth Initiative (BNI) which asks all leading corporations, institutions, commissions, universities, agencies, and bureaucratic groups, plus federal, provincial, municipal, territorial, and municipal governments to pledge to end anti-Black systemic racism by committing to the seven distinct goals outlined at BlackNorth.ca. The basic premise is that the Black talent is here, so let's use it. There is a commitment to certain hiring goals, such as hiring at least 5 percent of the student workforce from the Black community. This is a powerful, commendable initiative under excellent guidance from Wes and his executive team.

Thanks to the BNI, the Public Service of Canada and corporate Canada were finally beginning to see the need to create business opportunities for Black people. As part of the pledge, corporations and bureaucrats admit that the persistent inequities across Canada underscore the urgent, national need to address and alleviate racial, ethnic, and other tensions, and to eliminate anti-Black systemic racism wherever it exists. One of the ways the BNI wants to achieve that is to build a symbolic pipeline to facilitate representation from the Black community across Canada on boards of directors and among senior executives. The numeric goal is to have, at a minimum, 3.5 percent of executive and board roles based in Canada held by Black leaders by 2025. Hundreds of large Canadian corporations have signed the pledge and have started to work on proving the business case for diversity. That diversity can include Blacks, too!

BNI has the potential to be a real change agent. It has a powerful base consisting of some of Canada's leading corporations and senior bureaucrats. I was honoured to be asked to join the board and I was appointed chair of the public relations and public sector committee. In many ways, my involvement with BNI is the fulfillment of my life's work and my dream to break down systemic barriers and prove the business case for diversity. The design and approach of BNI eliminates that constant reminder I am different from most other Canadians. With BNI, I no longer feel that I must prove that I am worthy to participate in and enjoy all the fruits that have been bestowed on the white majority because of white privilege. BNI has taken a wonderfully holistic approach to the problem, and I believe it is going to work. I can see that some positive and some permanent things will flow from the BNI engagement. I encourage all Canadians to give them the strong support they deserve. Every bit counts.

Chapter 15

THE LATE EVENING OF LIFE

SO, HERE I AM, SIX YEARS AFTER LEARNING I HAD SIX MONTHS to live, writing the end of my memoir. I've fooled death, but I'm now probably living on borrowed time. My life has really changed. I cannot walk well and it is impossible to go anywhere without a cane or my walker. Peripheral neuropathy has taken over my feet, legs, hands, and fingers. I cannot safely operate a motor vehicle so I had to hire a driver. I cannot golf, garden, or work. I look out my windows and see my Christmas tree plantation, but I cannot work on it. I can't travel to give lectures. I spent February 2021, Black History Month, at home. I gave no speeches. I had no conferences to attend. I am just doing what I can do.

But out of darkness has come light. I have learned to accept all my limitations by turning all the good energy around me into an appreciation of the beauty and peace, that, frankly, I never saw before. I was always too busy. This has given me an opportunity to share with you some of the love and joy I receive from the farm, which is so similar to, yet so different from, my boyhood family farm in Wolfville.

There is a stillness and a quiet calm that is overwhelmingly comforting now that I am at peace. If you ever achieve this unique and rare state, it will be as though you have achieved the pinnacle of life—happy and content in blissful solitude. It's like time has stopped. All noise is gone. Not a sound can be heard. There's not even a whisper from the wind. Negativity is non-existent. This state is like being wrapped in an eiderdown quilt while gazing out a window in February, watching the falling snow as it is hurled and blown around by the howling winds. Icy outside, warm inside.

But there is no denying that old age and concomitant illness have set in. I have a whole series of new aches and mysterious pains. My heart, lungs, kidneys, and all the essential body organs are growing old and tired. They are not functioning well. My knee and hip joints are painfully not what they used to be. It's no longer easy to walk without mechanical aids, or to even hear family, neighbours, and close friends speak without the aid of little devices in both ears to amplify the sounds. It's becoming increasingly difficult to sustain my concentration while engaged in an interesting conversation with an old friend on current global affairs. My memories and recall mechanisms are being stretched to the limits. My attention span is like the tiny space between day and night, and it is waning, too.

I can recall times when I've been on a river fishing, or walking in the woods, as day slowly fades into night. It's odd, I know, but nature follows a formal pattern for that transition. The sun fades quickly in the west. The birds and crickets stop chirping and singing.

And suddenly, there is a solemn stillness. A nothingness. It is not quite night, but it's getting darker and darker by the second. For an instant, night and day are one. Life and death are one.

But I am still walking in the late evening of life. After a rainy few days, the bright full sun came out today and it was accompanied by pastel blue skies punctuated with white clouds of mysterious sizes and shapes—a wonder to observe over a tea and scone. These are all hints of the good life. I dreamed of days like this when I was working long, hard days, and even longer weekends. Now, it's the only thing on my bucket list. Just give me some quiet bliss so I can see, appreciate, and enjoy all the beauty of nature around me.

My Pleasant River farm is a little bit of heaven. It's not just a place to grow vegetables and flowers. It's a peaceful country estate with pristine charm and quiet beauty. To the east of the property is the Pleasant River itself, quietly meandering along the two hundred–acre property for about a mile through forests and meadows teeming with birds, rabbits, and deer. In the middle, surrounded by hayfields, stands my large century home, which has been elegantly restored and exudes country charm. The fields aren't there just to grow hay or oats. They are where nature displays herself in all her splendour and glory each day, revealing something different in every hour.

In recent weeks I have been spending a lot of time in my den on the second floor and in the solarium on the first floor. In late October, the acorns on the oak trees were maturing and offering themselves as delightful food for a variety of nature's creatures, large and small. Looking out the window from my favourite seat I started to see a lot of beautiful blue jays very busy at work in the trees. I had never been a bird watcher, but over the years while sitting on the back deck in the summer and having lunch, I have seen robins, hummingbirds, crows, owls, ravens, hawks, eagles, goldfinches, northern cardinals, and woodpeckers. I had never before really noticed the blue jays. There had not been any from April through August, but in the fall they were suddenly busy gathering food, eating grubs, bugs, and seeds, and making an odd assortment of musical sounds as they went about their business.

I've been studying the three big old oak trees off to the north. Recently, amid the heavy crop of acorns, I watched a few small blue jays with beautiful blue plumage pick up acorns in their beaks and start to pound them on a branch of the tree. They pounded and banged until the hard shells fell off; they would then eat the nut. As they ate, they made high-pitched hollering sounds, which attracted other birds. Soon there were ten, then twenty, and once I counted thirty birds. Each one swooping in, picking an acorn, and banging away until it opened. The birds flew at the tree with such a flourish that I often saw green leaves falling to the ground. Sometimes one nut would accidentally fall to the ground and the birds would swoop in and sweep it up. In all my years at the farm, I had never seen that before.

I've also been watching and listening to hummingbirds with their red and orange—and sometimes even avocado-coloured—plumage. They poke their long beaks deep into the summer flowers to extract nectar. They love our hollyhocks and make many furtive visits a day. They frequent my row of day lilies and explore the fox-gloves. The jet-like sound of their rapidly beating wings often gives me the sensation I am being dive-bombed, and in retrospect, I'm so glad no one else has been around to see me ducking awkwardly to dodge a darting hummingbird. When I'm really quiet, I can often hear them chirping. For a tiny bird, they certainly can make lots of noise! All of this is a great thrill.

I've witnessed some sad bird incidents, though. Once, I heard an incredible racket and saw seven crows, all cawing loudly, clacking their beaks to make an eerie sound. Then I spotted the gory spectacle causing the frenzy. A brown hawk had caught a baby crow in its sharp claws. The chick was about to become today's meal. As the baby struggled to live, the crows cawed angrily, and fought to free the baby. The hawk drove the crows off and the standoff continued. The hawk didn't move. The crows didn't leave. Life and death hung in the balance. Finally, the hawk burst into the air, prey in its claw, and vanished into the distance. I felt a rush of sorrow. I was amazed at the apparent affection these birds had for the chick. I also learned that the hawk, like the owl, is the bird to fear.

And now I cast my eyes over the fields and forests. There are no high-rise buildings in sight. Being here gives me a wonderful sense of freedom and joy. I add a day and a day and a day to my life. I'm sure some Canadians would rather spend their closing months amid the distracting din of a city. To each their own. This works well for me. I am content to sit, watch the natural world, and meditate on the words of poet Andrew Marvell through my last days:

> But at my back I always hear
> Time's winged chariot hurrying near,
> And yonder all before us lie
> Deserts of vast eternity.

I'm ready.

APPENDIX A

SIR GEORGE WILLIAMS UNIVERSITY SETTLEMENT AGREEMENT,
Students' Position, drafted by Donald Oliver, February 1969

On condition that the Administration of Sir George Williams University meet and fulfill our obligations as set forth in paragraph "B" hereof we the undersigned complainants do hereby agree to concurrently fulfill the following obligations:

1. Withdraw forthwith from occupation of the computer centre on the ninth floor of Sir George Williams University.
2. Undertake that those occupying portions of the seventh floor of the Sir George Williams University shall withdraw from occupation thereof forthwith.
3. Undertake that no violence will be directed towards Professor Perry Anderson during the negotiation of the settlement of the above affair.
4. Participate in the drafting and publication of a communiqué that will expressly state that negotiations are actively underway designed to create a hearing committee acceptable to all parties. Just 3 paragraphs from the University commitments should demonstrate the general trust of the intended obligation.
5.1. The Administration of Sir George Williams University hereby expressly declares and undertakes that the University shall do

all that is reasonably possible in the circumstances to assist Black students to make up time lost on courses during hearing of the Anderson affair, and specifically, but not to limit the generality of the foregoing, to extend time during which labs, assignments, and term papers must be submitted.

5.2 The University shall forthwith undertake to establish a new committee for hearing the charge of racism against Professor Anderson which committee shall be composed of two nominees by the Black students which nominees shall be non-negotiable, two from the other parties concerned non-negotiable, a fifth to be negotiated by all parties concerned, with each party maintaining the right to veto of the fifth, or any other form of committee that is mutually acceptable.

5.3. All parties to the proposed new committee shall be chosen and approved no later than February 15th. The final hearing shall commence on or before February 22nd, 1969.

ACKNOWLEDGEMENTS

UNLIKE MOST ACKNOWLEDGEMENTS PAGES, THIS ONE DOES not have a long list of people who encouraged me, supported me, or even gave a word-by-word critique of what I produced. That is because I did not tell a lot of people I was writing a book, because I did not want to build up expectations I could not fulfil on account of my illness. I did not know if I would be well enough to finish it.

Christopher Eyton, a good friend from Toronto, had given me a lot of helpful advice and several good suggestions over the years, but I did not even tell him for the same reason. Indeed, I did not tell even him until after the manuscript was in the hands of the publisher, but I do want to thank him sincerely for his perseverance and encouragement over many years.

If you knew them in person you would not be surprised to hear that I am most deeply indebted to my family, particularly Linda and Carolynn, for their encouragement, advice, comments, and frank editing suggestions, which opened my eyes to structural and other issues I had overlooked. In Linda's case, I cannot think of any act or series of acts that have helped me more in our forty-year marriage than the way she rolled up her sleeves and spent days and nights reading, editing, and writing notes for me on text. I think she sensed, correctly, that I was beginning to fade and did not have the strength and perseverance I once had. When I think about the depth of her help, I've been so moved that I've shed more than one tear of thanks in the quiet of my den. Thank you, Linda.

Carolynn had a full-time job in Fort St. John, British Columbia, but could always find the time to give me a critical, dead-on analysis in three or four sentences that spelled out clearly the hurdles I needed to overcome. She had a sense of sequencing of paragraphs that was very useful to this project.

I also explained to Carolynn how, on three separate occasions during this book process, Linda took the entire manuscript, printed it double-spaced, grabbed a lead pencil and a red pen, and proceeded to give the words a good massage. It took her hours and hours but it was worth it to me, because she picked up countless contradictions, repetitions, misspellings, incomplete sentences, and issues of syntax that saved the day before it reached the publishers.

Special thanks go out as well to my sisters Shirley and Nancy for their advice and information on family, and for encouraging me to go on with it. From a technical point of view on how we got this old rusty writing engine to start, I give thanks to Jon Tattrie for reading my rough manuscript, then writing out five or six probing questions about what was missing or what I had overwritten, which I then had to respond to with some serious thinking and rewriting. Those short, penetrating, searching questions were extremely useful to me.

I am deeply indebted to the Right Honourable Brian Mulroney for kindly agreeing to read the manuscript and write a foreword for the book. It is truly an honour when one of Canada's best prime ministers agrees, notwithstanding an incredibly heavy workload, to be associated in such a major way with my autobiography. It was his appointment of me to the Senate of Canada that provided me with the incentive and the authority to apply myself vigorously to promoting tolerance and diversity in Canada. Anything good that came from the second half of my life has to be attributed to the prime minister and his willingness to take a chance on me. After all, he had a lot of other choices for that appointment—many of whom were lined up and knocking on his door! Thank you, sir.

Finally, I want to say a special thanks to Whitney Moran and the Nimbus team for being so willing to help, and for their professionalism through this process. I was worried about my health, particularly because one of my close friends from Texas, a Black man with the same disease, the same doctors at the Mayo Clinic, and the same medication and treatment, recently died quite suddenly. He was younger than me. Nimbus agreed to the publishing timeline so we could have this in bookstores before my eighty-third birthday. And a warm, special thanks to Angela Mombourquette, Nimbus's non-fiction editor, for her exceptional editing and helpful suggestions, and her professionalism throughout.

–Don Oliver, July 2021